WITHDRAWN

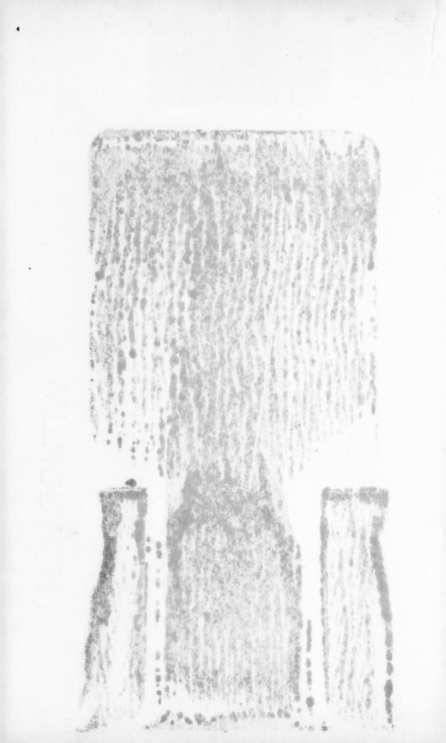

THE SPICE OF LIFE

CHRISTENDOM
IN DUBLIN

— + —

"So careful of the Type she seems":
  She mends what Man so foully makes:
Searching for five minute misprints
  In a forest of mistakes.

FF F (in form) dictated this
  You will agree, at any rate,
Some things are here which you believe
  And I did not Dictate.

As you were better than a friend
  In more than friendship we agree
Friendship at best may be a bond:
  And Truth has made us free.

Who enters by that Door alone,
  However dubious or afraid
For that one hour is that one Mind
  For which the World was made..

...So let them blare... Greed, rack and rod
  Torture and Torquemada's chain...
...That was the hour when souls were free
  That now are friends again —

To the Editor
Inscription in a copy of *Christendom in Dublin*
presented by G.K.C. to Dorothy Collins, 1932.

THE SPICE OF LIFE
AND OTHER ESSAYS

by

G. K. CHESTERTON

Edited by

DOROTHY COLLINS

1964
DARWEN FINLAYSON
BEACONSFIELD

First published 1964
by Darwen Finlayson Limited
Beaconsfield, Bucks.

Set in 11 on 12pt Baskerville
PRINTED IN GREAT BRITAIN BY
COX AND WYMAN, LTD.
LONDON, FAKENHAM AND READING

These essays cover a wide range of time and source. *The Spice of Life* was written only three months before G. K. Chesterton died. None of them has appeared in a collection before.

D. E. C.

CONTENTS

CONTENTS

THE ESSAY by G. K. Chesterton.

THE ESSAY is the only literary form which confesses, in its very name, that the rash act known as writing is really a leap in the dark. When men try to write a tragedy, they do not call the tragedy a try-on. Those who have toiled through the twelve books of an epic, writing it with their own hands, have seldom pretended that they have merely tossed off an epic as an experiment. But an essay, by its very name as well as its very nature, really is a try-on and really is an experiment. A man does not really write an essay. He does really essay to write an essay. One result is that, while there are many famous essays, there is fortunately no model essay. The perfect essay has never been written, for the simple reason that the essay has never really been written. Men have tried to write something, to find out what it was supposed to be. In this respect the essay is a typically modern product and is full of the future and the praise of experiment and adventure. In itself it remains somewhat elusive, and I will own that I am haunted with a faint suspicion that the essay will probably become rather more cogent and dogmatic, merely because of the deep and deadly divisions which ethical and economic problems may force upon us. But let us hope there will always be a place for the essay that is really an essay. St. Thomas Aquinas, with his usual common sense, said that neither the active nor the contemplative life could be lived without relaxation, in the form of jokes and games. The drama or the epic might be called the active life of literature; the sonnet or the ode the contemplative life. The essay is the joke.

Extract from introductory essay by G. K. Chesterton to Essays of the Year. See pp. 173–5 for all sources.

SENTIMENTAL LITERATURE

WE SHALL never attain to a serious and complete school of criticism so long as the word 'sentimental' is regarded as a term of depreciation. That 'passionate' should be a complimentary form and 'sentimental' a hostile one is as utterly unmeaning and ridiculous as it would be if 'blue' were complimentary and 'green' hostile. The difference between passion and sentiment is not, as is so often assumed, a difference in sincerity or wholesomeness or reality of feeling. It is a difference between two ways of looking at the same unquestionable facts of life. True sentiment consists in taking the central emotions of life not as passion takes them, personally, but impersonally, with a certain light and open confession of them as things common to us all. Passion is always a secret; it cannot be confessed; it is always a discovery; it cannot be shared. But sentiment stands for that frame of mind in which all men admit, with a half-humorous and half-magnanimous weakness, that they all possess the same secret, and have all made the same discovery. *Romeo and Juliet*, for example, is passionate. *Love's Labour's Lost* is sentimental. No man, perhaps, was more sentimental than Thackeray; a certain kind of cynicism is akin to sentiment in that it treats the emotions openly and lightly. To the man of passion, love and the world are new; to the man of sentiment they are infinitely old.

It is absolutely necessary to have some such clear idea as this in our heads before we can do justice to the immense flood of sentimentalism which is one of the heaviest items in the actual output of popular literature. If sentimental

literature is to be condemned it must emphatically not be because it is sentimental, it must be because it is not literature.
To complain that such literature is sultry and relaxing, that it
melts the character for a time into mere receptivity, that it
has scarcely more practical nourishment in it than the sugar
off a wedding-cake – to say all this is to complain that
Othello is tragic or that the *Mikado* degenerates into frivolity.
Sentimentality ought not to be anything but a passing mood;
people who are sentimental day and night are among the
most atrocious of the enemies of society. Dealing with them is
like seeing an interminable number of poetical sunsets going
on in the early morning. If sentimental literature is a curse,
it is not so much because it is read widely, as because it is
read exclusively.

There is a certain class of human feelings which must be
indulged, but which must not be trusted; to deny them is to
become a prig, but to confide in them is to cease to be a man.
There has, for example, arisen of late years in literature and
philosophy that craving for the strong man which is the mark
of weakness. To jeer at the philosophy of force and supre-
macy would be abominable, it would be like jeering at
biliousness or toothache. One of the most brilliant men of the
nineteenth century was the philosopher of force and supre-
macy, Nietzsche, and he died in a madhouse. There have
been many things, friendly and hostile, said about Nietzsche's philosophy, but few so far have pointed out the basic
fact that it is sentimental. It yields utterly to one of the
oldest, most generous, and most excusable of the weaknesses
of humanity, the hunger for the strong man. If any of
Nietzsche's followers wish to find the fullest and heartiest
acceptance of their master's doctrines, the most unrestrained
prostration before masculine pride and violence, they will
always find it in the novelettes. In these slight and periodical
forms of sentimental fiction we find pre-eminently developed
the tendency to give to the hero that kind of humour which

dishonours the giver. Just as nations crown their despots in their periods of weakness, so human nature in its periods of weakness craves for despots, more than it ever craved for liberty. It is a foolish feeling, and, perhaps an immoral one, but it has one quality which may slightly interest us, it is absolutely universal: nor are the most advanced or intellectual of mankind in this respect one scrap less sentimental than the rest.

Indeed, there are, perhaps no circles in which women are so sentimental and subservient as in unconventional circles. The tendency which leads the popular novelette to deify mere arrogance and possession is emphatically one of those kindly sins which must be repudiated without being despised. It is Literary Imperialism, and it is as old as the fear of life, which is older and much wiser than the fear of death. To the same class as this idolatry of bone or brain belongs the idolatry of title or class or calling, which is exhibited in sentimental literature. It is snobbish, and it is a snobbishness which is vital as the blood, and seems almost as old as the stars. It is vulgar, but this kind of vulgarity at least fulfils its name, and is indeed common. The problem of sentimental literature is the problem of whether there must not be somewhere an outlet for these follies which one would call pardonable if they did not seem too mighty and eternal to be pardoned. It is the problem whether one must not expect that people will be sentimental if they are neither old enough nor wise enough to be passionate.

This much, then, can be said about the vices of popular sentimentalism: that at least they are old and wholesome vices. Sentimentality, which it is fashionable to call morbid, is of all things most natural and healthy; it is the very extravagance of youthful health. Whatever may be said against the novelettes and serials which foster the profound sentimentalism of the man in the street, there is no count against them which bears any resemblance to the heavy responsibility of the polished and cynical fiction fashionable among the educated class. It does not bring into the world new sins or sinister levities or passions at once savage and artificial. The novelette may basely grovel before strength, but at least it does not basely grovel before weakness. It may speak openly and without reticence of emotions that are sacred and should be kept in the heart, but at least it does not speak openly and without reticence of emotions that are despicable and should be spewed out of the mouth. Its snobbery and autocracy are kindlier than many forms of emancipation; it is at least human even where it fails to be humane.

And of its merits there is surely something to be said: that the tired sempstress or the overworked shopgirl should only have as it were to open a door and find herself in a new room in which new and outrageously elegant figures are performing new and outrageously dignified actions is a gift that outweighs many stories of magic. That the actions of the figures are singularly languid and inevitable, that the characters are endowed with a very simple stock of virtues and vices, that the morality of the story is never for a moment mingled or perplexed, that over the whole scene broods the presence of an utterly fatalistic optimism, all this only makes the matter richer and quieter for tired intellects and tortured nerves.

That these dreams sometimes lead the dreamers to exaggerate and blunder, to overestimate or to underestimate life, may well be. The same troubles arose in connection with Christianity, that stupendous triumph of sentiment. Christianity also has led the weak, who were its care, to expect both too much and too little of life. But the supreme fact remains, that we can never estimate the value of a dream; that we can never know whether the ascetics, who drugged themselves with visions and scourged themselves with rods, were not the happiest of all the children of men.

HOW TO WRITE A DETECTIVE STORY

Let it be understood that I write this article as one wholly conscious that he has failed to write a detective story. But I have failed a good many times. My authority is therefore practical and scientific, like that of some great statesman or social thinker dealing with Unemployment or the Housing Problem. I do not pretend that I have achieved the ideal that I set up here for the young student; I am, if you will, rather the awful example for him to avoid. None the less I believe that there are ideals of detective writings, as of everything else worth doing; and I wonder they are not more often set out in all that popular didactic literature which teaches us how to do so many things so much less worth doing; as, for instance, how to succeed. Indeed, I wonder very much that the title at the top of this article does not stare at us from every bookstall. Pamphlets are published teaching people all sorts of things that cannot possibly be learnt, such as personality, popularity, poetry, and charm. Even those parts of literature and journalism that most obviously cannot be learnt are assiduously taught. But here is a piece of plain straightforward literary craftsmanship, constructive rather than creative, which could to some limited extent be taught and even, in very lucky instances, learnt. Sooner or later I suppose the want will be supplied, in that commercial system in which supply immediately answers to demand, and in which everybody seems to be thoroughly dissatisfied and unable to get anything he wants. Sooner or later, I suppose, there will not only be text-books teaching criminal investigators, but text-books teaching criminals. It will be but a slight change from the present tone of financial ethics, and when the shrewd and vigorous business mind has broken away from the last lingering influence of dogmas invented by priests, journalism and advertisement will show the same indifference to the taboos of today as does today to the taboos of the Middle Ages. Burglary will be explained like usury, and there will be no more disguise about cutting throats than there is about cornering markets. The bookstalls will be brightened with titles like 'Forgery in Fifteen Lessons,' and 'Why Endure Married Misery?' with a popularization of poisoning fully as scientific as the popularization of Divorce and Birth-Control.

But, as we are so often reminded, we must not be in a hurry for the arrival of a happy humanity; and meanwhile, we seem to be quite as likely to get good advice about committing crimes as good advice about detecting them, or about describing how they could be detected. I imagine the explanation is that the crime, the detection, the description, and the description of the description, do all demand a certain slight element of thought, while succeeding and writing a book on success in no way necessitate this tiresome experience. Anyhow, I find in my own case that when I begin to think of the theory of detective stories, I do become what some would call theoretical. That is, I begin at the beginning, without any pep, snap, zip or other essential of the art of arresting the attention, without in any way disturbing or awakening the mind.

The first and fundamental principle is that the aim of a mystery story, as of every other story and every other mystery, is not darkness but light. The story is written for the moment when the reader does understand, not merely for the many preliminary moments when he does not understand. The misunderstanding is only meant as a dark outline of cloud to bring out the brightness of that instant of intelligibility; and most bad detective stories are bad because they fail upon this point. The writers have a strange notion that it is their business to baffle the reader; and that so long as they baffle him it does not matter if they disappoint him. But it is not only necessary to hide a secret, it is also necessary to have a secret; and to have a secret worth hiding. The climax must not be an anti-climax; it must not merely consist of leading the reader a dance and leaving him in a ditch. The climax must not be only the bursting of a bubble but rather the breaking of a dawn; only that the daybreak is accentuated by the dark. Any form of art, however trivial, refers back to some serious truths; and though we are dealing with nothing more momentous than a mob of Watsons, all watching with round eyes like owls, it is still permissible to insist that it is the people who sat in darkness who have seen a great light; and that the darkness is only valuable in making vivid a great light in the mind. It always struck me as an amusing coincidence that the best of the Sherlock Holmes stories bore, with a totally different application and significance, a title that might have been invented to express this primal illumination; the title of "Silver Blaze".

The second great principle is that the soul of detective fiction is not complexity but simplicity. The secret may appear complex, but it must be simple; and in this also it is a symbol of higher mysteries. The writer is there to explain the mystery; but he ought not to be needed to explain the explanation. The explanation should explain itself; it should be something that can be hissed (by the villain, of course) in a few whispered words or shrieked preferably by the heroine before she swoons under the shock of the belated realization that two and two make four. Now some literary detectives make the solution more complicated than the mystery, and the crime more complicated than the solution.

Thirdly, it follows that so far as possible the fact or figure explaining everything should be a familiar fact or figure.

The criminal should be in the foreground, not in the capacity of criminal, but in some other capacity which nevertheless gives him a natural right to be in the foreground. I will take as a convenient case the one I have already quoted; the story of Silver Blaze. Sherlock Holmes is as familiar as Shakespeare; so there is no injustice by this time in letting out the secret of one of the first of these famous tales. News is brought to Sherlock Holmes that a valuable race-horse has been stolen, and the trainer guarding him murdered by the thief. Various people, of course, are plausibly suspected of the theft and murder; and everybody concentrates on the serious police problem of who can have killed the trainer. The simple truth is that the horse killed him. Now I take that as a model because the truth is so very simple. The truth really is so very obvious.

At any rate, the point is that the horse is very obvious. The story is named after the horse; it is all about the horse; the horse is in the foreground all the time, but always in another capacity. As a thing of great value he remains for the reader the Favourite; it is only as a criminal that he is a dark horse. It is a story of theft in which the horse plays the part of the jewel until we forget that the jewel can also play the part of the weapon. That is one of the first rules I would suggest, if I had to make rules for this form of composition. Generally speaking, the agent should be a familiar figure in an unfamiliar function. The thing that we realize must be a thing that we recognize; that is it must be something previously known, and it ought to be something prominently displayed. Otherwise there is no surprise in mere novelty. It is useless for a thing to be unexpected if it was not worth expecting. But it should be prominent for one reason and responsible for another. A great part of the craft or trick of writing mystery stories consists in finding a convincing but misleading reason for the prominence of the criminal, over and above his legitimate business of committing the crime.

Many mysteries fail merely by leaving him at loose ends in the story, with apparently nothing to do except to commit the crime. He is generally well off, or our just and equal law would probably have him arrested as a vagrant long before he was arrested as a murderer. We reach the stage of suspecting such a character by a very rapid if unconscious process of elimination. Generally we suspect him merely because he has not been suspected. The art of narrative consists in convincing the reader for a time, not only that the character might have come on the premises with no intention to commit a felony, but that the author has put him there with some intention that is not felonious. For the detective story is only a game; and in that game the reader is not really wrestling with the criminal but with the author.

What the writer has to remember, in this sort of game, is that the reader will not say, as he sometimes might of a serious or realistic study: "Why *did* the surveyor in green spectacles climb the tree to look into the lady doctor's back garden?" He will insensibly and inevitably say, "Why did the author *make* the surveyor climb a tree, or introduce any surveyor at all?" The reader may admit that the town would in any case need a surveyor, without admitting that the tale would in any case need one. It is necessary to explain his presence in the tale (and the tree) not only by suggesting why the town council put him there, but why the author put him there. Over and above any little crimes he may intend to indulge in, in the inner chamber of the story, he must have already some other justification as a character in a story and not only as a mere miserable material person in real life. The instinct of the reader, playing hide-and-seek with the writer, who is his real enemy, is always to say with suspicion, "Yes, I know a surveyor might climb a tree; I am quite aware that there are trees and that there are surveyors, but what are you doing with them? Why did you make this particular surveyor climb this particular tree in this particular tale, you cunning and evil-minded man?"

This I should call the fourth principle to be remembered, as in the other cases, people probably will not realize that it is practical, because the principles on which it rests sound theoretical. It rests on the fact that in the classification of the arts, mysterious murders belong to the grand and joyful company of the things called jokes. The story is a fancy; an avowedly fictitious fiction. We may say if we like that it is a very artificial form of art. I should prefer to say that it is professedly a toy, a thing that children 'pretend' with. From this it follows that the reader, who is a simple child and therefore very wide awake, is conscious not only of the toy but of the invisible playmate who is the maker of the toy, and the author of the trick. The innocent child is very sharp and not a little suspicious. And one of the first rules I repeat, for the maker of a tale that shall be a trick, is to remember that the masked murderer must have an artistic right to be on the scene and not merely a realistic right to be in the world. He must not only come to the house on business, but on the business of the story; it is not only a question of the motive of the visitor but of the motive of the author. The ideal mystery story is one in which he is such a character as the author would have created for his own sake, or for the sake of making the story move in other necessary matters, and then be found to be present there, not for the obvious and sufficient reason, but for a second and a secret one. I will add that for this reason, despite the sneers at 'love-interest' there is a good deal to be said for the tradition of sentiment and slower or more Victorian narration. Some may call it a bore, but it may succeed as a blind.

Lastly the principle that the detective story like every literary form starts with an idea, and does not merely start out to find one, applies also to its more material mechanical detail. Where the story turns upon detection, it is still

necessary that the writer should begin from the inside,
though the detective approaches from the outside. Every
good problem of this type originates in a positive notion,
which is in itself a simple notion; some fact of daily life that
the writer can remember and the reader can forget. But anyhow, a tale has to be founded on a truth; and though
opium may be added to it, it must not merely be an opium
dream.

HUMOUR

HUMOUR, in the modern use of the term, signifies a perception of the comic or incongruous of a special sort; generally distinguished from Wit, as being on the one side more subtle, or on the other side more vague. It is thus a term which not only refuses to be defined, but in a sense boasts of being indefinable; and it would commonly be regarded as a deficiency in humour to search for a definition of humour. The modern use of the term, however, is by no means the primary or necessary use of it; and it is one of the cases, rarer than is commonly supposed, in which derivation offers at least an approach to definition. Everybody knows that 'Humor', in the Latin sense of 'moisture' was applied here as part of the old physiological theory, by which the characters of men varied according to the proportions of certain different secretions in the human body; as, for instance, that the predominance of phlegm produced the phlegmatic humour. By the time of the full consolidation of the English language, it had thus become possible for Ben Jonson and others to use the word 'humour' rather in the sense of 'the ruling passion'. With this there necessarily went an idea of exaggeration; and by the end of the process the character of a humorist was more or less identical with what we should call an eccentric. The next stages of the development, which are rather slow and subtle correspond to the various degrees in which the eccentric has become conscious of his eccentricity. England has always been especially rich in these eccentrics; and in England, where everything was less logical and more casual than in other countries, the eccentric long remained, as we should say, half unconsciously and half consciously humorous. The blend, and the beginnings of the modern meaning, may perhaps be dated at about the time of Walter Scott's Waverley Novels; when Guy Mannering complains of Councillor Pleydell as 'a crack-brained humorist'. For Pleydell is indeed laughed at for his little vanities or whims; but he himself joins in the laugh and sees the humour of his humour. Since then the word has come to be used more and more exclusively of conscious humour; and generally of a rather deep and delicate appreciation of the absurdities of others.

Nevertheless there clings to the word Humour, especially when balanced against the word Wit, a sort of tradition or atmosphere that belongs to the old eccentrics whose eccentricity was always wilful and not infrequently blind. The distinction is a fine one; but one of the elements remaining in this blend is a certain sense of being laughed at, as well as of laughing. It involves some confession of human weakness; whereas wit is rather the human intellect exerting its full strength, though perhaps upon a small point. Wit is reason on its judgment seat; and though the offenders may be touched lightly, the point is that the judge is not touched at all. But humour always has in it some idea of the humorist himself being at a disadvantage and caught in the entanglements and contradictions of human life. It is a grave error to underrate Wit as something trivial; for certain purposes of satire it can truly be the sword of the spirit, and the satirist bears not the sword in vain. But it is essential to wit that he should bear the sword with ease; that for the wit the weapon should be light if the blow be heavy; that there should be no question of his being encumbered with his instrument or laying open his guard. But humour can be of the finest and yet lay open the guard or confess its inconsistency. When Voltaire said, commenting on the judicial murder of Byng, "In England they kill one Admiral to encourage the others," it would immediately be recognized as humour. But we rightly class Voltaire as a wit, because he represents the consistent human reason detesting an inconsistency. We shall be very wrong if we despise him as a wit, for that French clearness has depths of irony; there is, for instance, more than is seen at a glance in the very word 'encourage'. But it is true that the wit is here a judge independent of the judges, unaffected by the King or the Admiral or the English Court-martial or the mob. He is abstract justice recording a contradiction. But when Falstaff (a model of the humorist become or becoming conscious) cries out in desperate bravado, "They hate us youth," the incongruity between the speech and the corpulent old humbug of a speaker is present to his own mind, as well as to ours. He also discovers a contradiction, but it is in himself; for Falstaff really did bemuse himself with youthful companionship which he knew to be like a drug or a dream; and indeed Shakespeare himself, in one at least of the Sonnets, becomes bitterly conscious of the same illusion. There is therefore in humour, or at least in the origins of humour, something of this idea of the eccentric caught in the act of eccentricity and brazening it out; something of one surprised in disarray and become conscious of the chaos within. Wit corresponds to the divine virtue of justice, in so far as so dangerous a virtue can belong to man. Humour corresponds to the human virtue of humility and is only more divine because it has, for the moment, more sense of the mysteries.

If there be so much of enlightenment to be gathered from the history of the word, there is very little to be gathered from any of the attempts at a scientific history of the thing. The speculations on the nature of any reaction to the risible belong to the larger and more elementary subject of Laughter and are for the department of psychology; according to some, almost for that of physiology. Whatever be their value touching the primitive function of laughter, they throw very little light on the highly civilized product of humour. It may well

24

be questioned whether some of the explanations are not too crude even for the crudest origins; that they hardly apply even to the savage and certainly do not apply to the child. It has been suggested, for example, that all laughter had its origin in a sort of cruelty, in an exultation over the pain or ignominy of an enemy; but it is very hard even for the most imaginative psychologist to believe that, when a baby bursts out laughing at the image of the cow jumping over the moon, he is really finding pleasure in the probability of the cow breaking her leg when she comes down again. The truth is that all these primitive and prehistoric origins are largely un-known and possibly unknowable; and like all the unknown and unknowable are a field for furious wars of religion. Such primary human causes will always be interpreted differently according to different philosophies of human life. Another philosophy would say, for instance, that laughter is due not to an animal cruelty but to a purely human realization of the contrast between man's spiritual immensity within and his littleness and restriction without, for it is itself a joke that a house should be larger inside than out. According to such a view, the very incompatability between the sense of human dignity and the perpetual possibility of incidental indignities, produces the primary or archetypal joke of the old gentleman sitting down suddenly on the ice. We do not laugh thus when a tree or a rock tumbles down; because we do not know the sense of self-esteem or serious importance within. But such speculations in psychology, especially in primitive psycho-logy, have very little to do with the actual history of comedy as an artistic creation.

There is no doubt that comedy existed as an artistic creation many thousands of years ago, in the case of peoples whose life and letters we can sufficiently understand to appreciate the fine shades of meaning; especially, of course, in the case of the Greeks. It is difficult for us to say how far it existed in civilizations more remote of which the records are

for us more stiff and symbolic; but the very limitation of
symbolism which makes it hard for us to prove its existence
should warn us against assuming without evidence that it did
not exist. We know more about Greek humour than about
Hittite humour, at least partly for the simple reason that we
know Greek better than we know any sort of colloquial
Hittite; and while what applies to Hittite applies too in a less
degree to Hebrew, a case like that of early Hebrew presents
something of the same problem of limitation. But without
any attempts to settle such problems of scholarship, it is hard
to believe that the highest sense of human satire was not
present in the words of Job. "Truly you are wise and wisdom
will die with you"; or that no perception of a poetic contrast
was felt by so great a poet when he said of Behemoth, commonly identified with the hippopotamus; "Canst thou play
with him as with a bird?" It is probable that the Chinese
civilization, in which the quality of the quaint and the
fantastic has flowered with a beautiful luxuriance for many
centuries, could also quote fairly early examples of the same
order of fancy.

In any case, humour is in the very foundations of our
European literature, which alone is quite sufficiently a part
of ourselves for the full appreciation of so subtle and sometimes sub-conscious a quality. Even a schoolboy can see it in
such scenes of Aristophanes as that in which the dead man
sits up in indignation at having to pay the toll of the Styx,
and says he would rather come to life again; or when
Dionysus asks to see the wicked in hell and is answered by a
gesture pointing at the audience. Before the period of intellectual controversies in Athens, indeed, we generally find
in Greek poetry, as in the greater part of all human folk lore,
that the joke is a practical joke. To a robust taste, however, it
is none the less of a joke for that. For the joke of Odysseus
calling himself Noman is not, as some suppose, a sort of
trivial pun or verbalism; the joke is in the gigantic image of

26

the raging Cyclops, roaring as if to rend the mountains, after being defeated by something so simple and so small. And this example is worth noting; as representing what is really the fun of all the fairy-tales; the notion of something apparently omnipotent made impotent by some tiny trick. This fairy-tale idea is undoubtedly one of the primitive fountains from which flows the long winding stream of historic humour. When Puss in Boots persuades the boastful magician to turn into a mouse and be eaten, it almost deserves to be called wit.

After these two early expressions, the practical joke of the folk-tale and the more philosophic fun of the Old Comedy, the history of humour is simply the history of literature. It is especially the history of European literature; for this sane sense of the incongruous is one of the highest qualities balancing the European spirit. It would be easy to go through the rich records of every nation and note this element in almost every novel or play, and in not a few poems or philosophical works. There is naturally no space for such a survey; but three great names, one English, one French and a third Spanish, may be mentioned for their historical quality; since they opened new epochs and even their few superiors were still their followers. The first of these determining names is that of Chaucer, whose urbanity has done something to conceal his real originality. Medieval civilization had a very powerful sense of the grotesque, as is apparent in its sculpture alone; but it was in a sense a fighting sentiment; it dealt with dragons and devils; it was alive, but it was very decidedly kicking. Chaucer brought into this atmosphere a cool air of true comedy; a sort of incongruity most incongruous in that world. In his personal sketches we have a new and very English element, of at once laughing at people and liking them. The whole of humorous fiction, if not the whole of fiction, dates from the Prologue of the Canterbury Tales.

Rather later, Rabelais opened a new chapter by showing

that intellectual things could be treated with the energy of high spirits and a sort of pressure of physical exuberance, which was itself humorous in its very human abandon. He will always be the inspiration of a certain sort of genial impatience; and the moments when the great human mind boils over like a pot. The Renaissance itself was, of course, such a boiling, but the elements were some of them more poisonous; though a word should be said for the tonics of that time, the humour of Erasmus and of More. Thirdly, there appeared with the great Cervantes an element new in its explicit expression; that grand and very Christian quality of the man who laughs at himself. Cervantes was himself more chivalrous than most men when he began to mock at chivalry. Since his time, humour in this purely humorous sense, the confession of complexity and weakness already remarked upon, has been a sort of secret of the high culture of the West. The influence of Cervantes and Rabelais, and the rest runs through all modern letters, especially our own; taking on a shrewd and acid tang in Swift, a more delicate and perhaps more dubious taste in Sterne, passing on through every sort of experiment of essay or comedy, pausing upon the pastoral gaiety of Goldsmith or going on finally to bring forth, like a great birth of giants, the walking caricatures of Dickens. Nor is it altogether a national accident that the tradition has here been followed in our own nation. For it is true that humour, in the special and even limited sense here given to it, humour as distinct from wit, from satire, from irony or from many things that may legitimately produce amusement, has been a thing strongly and specially present in English life and letters. That we may not in turn depreciate the wit and logic of the rest of the world, it will be well to remember that humour does originate in the half-conscious eccentric, that it is in part a confession of inconsistency, but, when all is said, it has added a new beauty to human life. It may even be noted that there has appeared especially in England a new variety of humour, more properly to be called Nonsense. Nonsense may be described as humour which has for the moment renounced all connection with wit. It is humour that abandons all attempt at intellectual justification; and does not merely jest at the incongruity of some accident or practical joke, as a by-product of real life, but extracts and enjoys it for its own sake. Jabberwocky is not a parody on anything; the Jumblies are not a satire on anybody; they are folly for folly's sake on the same lines as art for art's sake, or more properly beauty for beauty's sake; and they do not serve any social purpose except perhaps the purpose of a holiday. Here again it will be well to remember that even the work of humour should not consist entirely of holidays. But this art of nonsense is a valuable contribution to culture; and it is very largely, or almost entirely, an English contribution. So cultivated and competent a foreign observer as M. Emile Cammaerts has remarked that it is so native as to be at first quite unmeaning to foreigners. This is perhaps the latest phase in the history of humour; but it will be well even in this case to preserve what is so essential a virtue of humour; the virtue of proportion. Humour, like wit, is related however indirectly, to truth and the eternal virtues; as it is the greatest incongruity of all to be serious about humour, so it is the worst sort of pomposity to be monotonously proud of humour; for it is itself the chief antidote to pride; and has been, ever since the time of the Book of Proverbs, the hammer of fools.

FICTION AS FOOD

I HAVE been asked to explain what I meant by saying that "Literature is a luxury; fiction is a necessity." I have no notion when I said it or where I said it, or even whether I said it; in the sense that I do not now remember ever saying it at all. But I do know why I said it; if I ever said it at all. That is the advantage of believing in what some call dogma and others call logic. Some people seem to imagine that a man being sceptical and changing his beliefs, or even a man being cynical and disregarding his beliefs, is a sort of advantage to him in liberality and flexibility of mind. The truth is exactly the other way. By the very laws of the mind, it is more difficult to remember disconnected things than connected things; and a man is much more in control of a whole range of controversy if he has connected beliefs than if he had never had anything but disconnected doubts. Therefore I can immediately understand the sentence submitted to me, as if it were a sentence made up by somebody else; as perhaps it was.

Literature is a luxury, because it is part of what is popularly called "having the best of everything". Matthew Arnold would have been pained to be called popular; but he said what is really the same thing as the popular saying; that Culture is knowing the best that has been said and thought. Literature is indeed one of those nobler luxuries which a well-governed state would extend to all, and even regard as necessities in that nobler sense. But it is a luxury in the plain sense that human beings can do without it and still be tolerably human, or even tolerably happy. But human beings cannot be human without some field of fancy or imagination; some vague idea of the romance of life; and even some holiday of the mind in a romance that is a refuge from life.

Every healthy person at some period must feed on fiction as well as fact; because fact is a thing which the world gives to him, whereas fiction is a thing which he gives to the world. It has nothing to do with a man being able to write; or even with his being able to read. Perhaps its best period is that of childhood, and what is called playing or pretending. But it is still true when the child begins to read or sometimes (heaven help him) to write. Anybody who remembers a favourite fairy-story will have a strong sense of its original solidity and richness and even definite detail; and will be surprised, if he re-reads it in later life, to find how few and bald were the words which his own imagination made not only vivid but varied. And even the errand-boy who reads hundreds of penny-dreadfuls, or the lady who read hundreds of novels from the circulating library, were living an imaginative life which did not come wholly from without.

Now nobody supposes that all those things which feed the hunger for fiction would commend themselves to the palate of literature. Literature is only that rare sort of fiction which rises to a certain standard of objective beauty and truth. When a child, almost as soon as he can speak, has invented the imaginary family of Pubbles, with father and mother and naughty child all complete, nobody supposes that the psychology of the house of Pubbles is differentiated as delicately as that of the family of Poynton, in a story by Henry James. When the lady has followed and forgotten a hundred heroines in their wanderings through mysterious suburban flats or murderous country rectories, nobody supposes that each of them remains even for her a portrait, as vivid as Elizabeth Bennet or Becky Sharp. It is not a thing like having an appreciation of a good wine; it is a thing like having an appetite for a square meal; it is not a vintage but a viand.

Now this general need is connected with the deepest things in man; and the strangest thing about him, which is being a man. As a large mirror will make one room look like two rooms, so the mind of man is from the first a double mind; a thing of reflection and living in two worlds at once. The cave-man who was not content that reindeers should be real – did something that no other animal ever has done or apparently ever will do. Of course, we cannot prove that the animal has not imagination in the inferior sense. For all we can prove, the rhinoceros may have an Invisible Playmate; and yet realize with his reason that "it is but a rhinoceros of air; that lingers in the garden there."

Scientifically speaking, we cannot demonstrate that the rabbit has not an imaginary family of rabbits, on the lines of Brer Rabbit, as well as the somewhat large and increasing family which the rabbit produces in the ordinary way of business. But there is such a thing as common sense; and I think our common sense inclines us to suppose that any such artistic daydream, if it exists in beasts and birds, is much more rudimentary and stationary; and has certainly never ad-vanced to the point of expression, even in fairy-tales or penny-dreadfuls. But for man some form of this fanciful experience is essential as a mere fact of experience. If he has not that daydream all his day, he is not man; and if he is not man, there is nobody to write about and nobody to write about him.

II

I was a great reader of novels until I began to review them. when I naturally left off reading them. I do not mean to admit that I did them any injustice; I studied and sampled them with the purpose of being strictly fair; but I do not call that 'novel reading' in the old enchanting sense. If I read them thoroughly I still read them rapidly; which is quite against my instincts for the mere luxury of reading. When I was a boy and really had a new adventure story, when I was a young man and read my first few detective stories, I did not enjoy precipitation, but actually enjoyed delay. The pleasure was so intense that I was always putting it off. For it is one of the two or three big blunders in modern morality to suppose that the strongest eagerness expresses itself in extravagance. The strongest eagerness always expresses itself in thrift. That is why the French Revolution was French and not English; why the careful peasants have turned the world upside-down, while the careless labourers have cheerfully left it as it was. When a child's soul is in the most starry ecstasy of greed he desires to have his cake, not to eat it. I am English myself, and I have never managed to be thrifty about anything else.

But about my early novel reading I was as thrifty as a French peasant – and as greedy. I loved to look at the mere solid bulk of a sensational novel as one looks at the solid bulk of a cheese; to open the first page, dally with the first paragraph, and then shut it again, feeling how little pleasure I had lost as yet. And my favourite novelists are still those great nineteenth-century novelists who give an impression of bewildering bulk and variety, Scott or Dickens or Thackeray. I have artistic pleasure as keen or keener, I have moral sympathy as intense or more intense with many later writers; with the hard-hitting *mot juste* of Stevenson's stories or the insurgent irony of Mr. Belloc's. But Stevenson has one fault as a novelist, that he must be read quickly. Novels like Belloc's *Mr. Burden* must not only be read quickly but fiercely; they describe a short, sharp struggle; the mood both of writer and reader is heroic and abnormal, like that of two men fighting a duel. But Scott, Thackeray, and Dickens had the mysterious trick or talent of the inexhaustible novel.

Even when we have come to the end of the story we some-how feel that it is endless. People say they have read *Pickwick* five times or fifty times or five hundred times. For my part I have only read *Pickwick* once. Since then I have lived in *Pickwick*; walked into it when and where I chose, as a man walks into his club. But whenever I have walked in, it seemed to me that I found something new. I am not sure that stringent modern artists like Stevenson or Mr. Belloc do not actually suffer from the strictness and swiftness of their art. If a book is a book to be lived in, it should be (like a house to be lived in) a little untidy.

Apart from such chaotic classics as these, my own taste in novel reading is one which I am prepared in a rather especial manner, not only to declare, but to defend. My taste is for the sensational novel, the detective story, the story about death, robbery and secret societies; a taste which I share in common with the bulk at least of the male population of this world. There was a time in my own melodramatic boyhood when I became quite fastidious in this respect. I would look at the first chapter of any new novel as a final test of its merits. If there was a murdered man under the sofa in the first chapter, I read the story. If there was no murdered man under the sofa in the first chapter, I dismissed the story as tea-table twaddle, which it often really was. But we all lose a little of that fine edge of austerity and idealism which sharpened our spiritual standard in our youth. I have come to compromise with the tea-table and to be less insistent about the sofa. As long as a corpse or two turns up in the second, the third, nay even the fourth or fifth chapter, I make allowance for human weakness, and I ask no more. But a novel without any death in it is still to me a novel without any life in it. I admit that the very best of the tea-table novels are great art – for instance, *Emma* or *Northanger Abbey*. Sheer elemental genius can make a work of art out of anything. Michelangelo might make a statue out of mud, and Jane Austen could make a novel out of tea – that much more contemptible substance. But on the whole I think that a tale about one man killing another man is more likely to have something in it than a tale in which, all the characters are talking trivialities without any of that instant and silent presence of death which is one of the strong spiritual bonds of all mankind. I still prefer the novel in which one person does another person to death to the novel in which all the persons are feebly (and vainly) trying to get the others to come to life.

But I have another and more important quarrel about the sensational novel. There seems to be a very general idea that the romance of the tomahawk will be (or will run the risk of being) more immoral than the romance of the teapot. This I violently deny. And in this I have the support of practically all the old moral traditions of our civilization and of every civilization. High or low, good or bad, clever or stupid, a moral story almost always meant a murderous story. For the old Greeks a moral play was one full of madness and slaying. For the great medievals a moral play was one which exhibited the dancing of the devil and the open jaws of hell. For the great Protestant moralists of the seventeenth and eighteenth centuries a moral story meant a story in which a parricide was struck by lightning or a boy was drowned for fishing on a Sunday. For the more rationalistic moralists of the eighteenth century, such as Hogarth, Richardson, and the author of *Sandford and Merton*, all agreed that shocking calamities could properly be indicated as the result of evil doing; that the more shocking those calamities were the more moral they were. It is only in our exhausted and agnostic age that the idea has been started that if one is moral one must not be melodramatic.

But I believe that sensational novels are the most moral part of modern fiction, and I believe it upon two converging lines, such as make all real conviction. It is, I think, the fact that melodramatic fiction is moral and not immoral. And it is, I think, the abstract truth that any literature that represents our life as dangerous and startling is truer than any literature that represents it as dubious and languid. For life is a fight and is not a conversation.

THE SOUL IN EVERY LEGEND

I THINK it was that very fine and subtle writer, Vernon Lee, who lapsed into literary heresy by saying that a poet is always a pantheist. I could only accept this in the amended form that no poet, by any possiblity, has ever been or ever will be a pantheist. It was precisely because Walt Whitman sometimes tried on principle to be a pantheist, that so great a genius just missed being a poet. Shelley did not miss being a poet; but he did miss being a pantheist. A deep imaginative instinct, beyond all his cheap philosophies, made him always do something which is the soul of imagination, but the very opposite of universalism. It made him *insulate* the object of which he wrote; making the cloud or the bird as solitary as possible in the sky. Imagination demands an image. An image demands a background. The background should be equal and level, or vast and vague, but only for the sake of the image. In writing of the skylark Shelley compares that unfortunate wild fowl to a lady in a tower, to a star, to a rose, to all sorts of things that are not in the least like a skylark. But they all have one touch, the touch of separation and solitude. Now pantheism means that nothing is thus separated; that the divine essence is equally distributed at any given moment in all the atoms of the universe; and that he who would see it imaginatively must see it as a whole. I deny that this was done by Shelley the poet; whatever may have been done by Shelley the prig. When he heard the skylark speaking to him like a spirit out of heaven, I deny that he heard at the same moment the crowing of cocks, the screaming of cockatoos, the gobbling of turkeys, the cawing of rooks, the clucking of hens and the pandemonium of the parrot-house at the Zoo; or that for him, at that moment, all these things mingled in one harmony or music of the spheres.

I do not deny that the poet may write an ode to a parrot as well as to a skylark; or for that matter a serenade to a penguin or a pelican. But he will prefer the parrot outside the parrot-house. He will prefer the pelican in the wilderness. In short, he will aim at seeing the object against a background, as one sees a star in the sky or an island in the sea. He will aim at seeing the object in the strict sense of *distinguishing* the object. And this element of distinction would alone distinguish such a poet from the vulgar universality of the ordinary pantheist. For the rest, Shelley's poetry very seldom expressed Shelley's philosophy. When once he began to sing, he generally sang the creeds that he refused to say. In the skylark, for instance, he does not in the least proclaim the doctrine of Universal Nature or the Immanence of God. What he does proclaim is the doctrine of Original Sin, or the Fall of Man. When the skylark ceases merely to flutter and begins really to fly, to sweep and to soar; when the verse takes on the swing and powerful pulsation of great poetry, it is not even about the isolation of the bird but the stranger isolation of the man. "We look before and after . . . our sweetest songs are those that tell of saddest thought."

> But if we could scorn
> Hate and pride and fear,
> If we were things born
> Not to shed a tear –

There the pantheistic poet is telling a tale not told by all the parrots in the Zoological Gardens; but rather by the Bird of Paradise that came with us out of the Garden of Eden.

Mr. Bernard Shaw, in a preface to one of his plays, advances a thesis in science and then propounds it as a thesis in philosophy. It might well be described as a progressive pantheism, as compared with the static pantheism more commonly associated with pantheists. The current criticism will probably be that it is all very well for Mr. Shaw to talk philosophy, but he knows nothing about science. To me this seems the exact contrary of the fact. He has always been very well equipped with facts in his scientific controversies; and his logic, of which I can judge better, seems to me very conclusive on the purely scientific question. He is strictly scientific in refusing the test of cutting off a mouse's tail, for instance, as affecting the question of acquired characteristics. As he very sensibly points out, an arbitrary amputation by somebody else is not an acquired characteristic at all; any more than we can talk of a man acquiring a railway accident. The Lamarckian suggestion is that the will counts; and nobody wills a railway accident. I think Mr. Shaw is entirely successful in his science; where I begin to doubt is precisely in his philosophy, and especially when he propounds it as a religion. And I doubt it because it ignores, as the more static pantheism ignores the same rather indescribable element which I can only call identity. I can only dimly describe it as the conviction that it is It.

Mr. Shaw suggests that we should all pool our legends and treat them all equally as legends; that is, as allegories. This, I fancy, is very much what was really done by the Neo-Platonists and other syncretists of the pagan sunset on the Mediterranean. They made a pool of all the legends; and it was rather a stagnant pool. Indeed the Mediterranean itself would henceforth have been little more than a stagnant pool, but for the wind of the spirit that blew on it from Bethlehem and Calvary; that is from real places alive with stories at least believed to be real. When the new world found something to follow, it had to be a man and not a myth, a tragedy and not a mummery. If the new world finds a new religion now, it is much more likely to be in Spiritualist miracles and

39

a Spiritualist plan of heaven and earth, all to be believed down to the last detail, than in the weary impartiality of the pool of the Neo-Platonists. That pool may be a sea into which all religions ultimately run. It is certainly not a spring in which any religions originally rise. We shall never make a new legend by advertising for an allegory. The great myth comes from men who believe they have found a great truth, at least at first and that a vivid and final truth. If there be, as I believe, such a central truth, this is the only way in which men can receive that truth. But even if it be only a delusion, this is the only way in which it can be denied.

In short, it is not enough for a religion to include everything. It must include everything and something over. That is it must include everything and include something as well. It must answer that deep and mysterious human demand for everything; even if the nature of that demand be too deep to be easily defined in logic. It will never cease to be described in poetry. We might almost say that all poetry is a description of it. Even when you have only natural religion, you will still have supernatural poetry. And it will be poetic because it is particular, not because it is general. The new priest may proclaim, "The sea is God, the land is God and the sky is God; but yet there are not three Gods, but one God." But even if the old priest be silenced, the old poet will always answer, "God is in a cave; God is in a stable; God is disguised and hidden. I alone know where he is; he is herding the cattle of Admetus; he is pouring out the wine of Cana." The new republic may make the philosophical declaration, "We hold these truths to be self-evident, that all trees were evolved equal and endowed with the dignity of creative evolution." But if in the silence that follows we overhear the poor nurse or the peasant mother telling fairy-tales to the children, she will always be saying, "And in the seventh garden beyond the seventh gate was the tree with the golden apples", or "They sailed and sailed till they came to an island, and in the island was a meadow, and in the meadow the tree of life."

Now according to the old rationalistic criticism, it was enough to say of a fancy that it was fanciful. It was enough to say that a religion was a romance, and a romance a delusion. But men like Mr. Shaw have already left that behind, in the years of wandering starting from the Dublin of the Protestants and the Darwin of the Professors. They already realized that there is "a soul in every dogma", that religion cannot be left out of account, that rationalism cannot be left in control. Now if we are to look sympathetically for the soul in every dogma, surely we must look for that something in the soul which makes it clothe itself in every case in a particular and personal body. If this particularism always stubbornly recurs even in poetry, how can it be left out of philosophy? What is the *meaning* of this incurable itch to give to airy nothing, or still more airy everything, a local habitation and a name? Why is it always something at once odd and objective, a precious fruit or a flying cup or a buried key, that symbolizes the mystery of the world? Why should not the world symbolize the world? Why should not a sphere sufficiently represent universalism; so that the faithful might be found adoring a plum-pudding or a cannon-ball? Why should not a spiral sufficiently represent progress; and the pious bow down before a corkscrew? In practice we know that it would be impossible to dissociate a Christmas pudding from the sacramental specialism of Christmas; and the worship of the corkscrew, that hieratic serpent, would probably be traced to the mysteries of Dionysius. In a word, *why* are all mysteries concerned with the notion of finding a particular thing in a particular place? If we are to find the real meaning of every element in mythology, what is the real meaning of *that* element in it? I can see only one possible answer that satisfies the new more serious and sympathetic study of religion, even among sceptics; and that is that there really is something to which all these fancies are what forgeries are to a signature; that if the soul could be satisfied with the truth it would find it a tale as particular, as positive and as personal; that the light which we follow first as a wide white star actually narrows as we draw nearer to it, till we find that trailing meteor is something like a light in a window or a candle in a room.

PART TWO: PARTICULAR BOOKS AND WRITERS

THE MACBETHS

In studying any eternal tragedy the first question necessarily is what part of tragedy is eternal. If there be any element in man's work which is in any sense permanent it must have this characteristic, that it rebukes first one generation and then another, but rebukes them always in opposite directions and for opposite faults. The ideal world is always sane. The real world is always mad. But it is mad about a different thing every time; all the things that have been are changing and inconstant. The only thing that is really reliable is the thing that has never been. All very great classics of art are a rebuke to extravagance not in one direction but in all directions. The figure of a Greek Venus is a rebuke to the fat women of Rubens and also a rebuke to the thin women of Aubrey Beardsley. In the same way, Christianity, which in its early years fought the Manicheans because they did not believe in anything but spirit, has now to fight the Manicheans because they do not believe in anything but matter. This is perhaps the test of a very great work of classic creation, that it can be attacked on inconsistent grounds, and that it attacks its enemies on inconsistent grounds. Here is a broad and simple test. If you hear a thing being accused of being too tall and too short, too red and too green, too bad in one way and too bad also in the opposite way, then you may be sure that it is very good.

This preface is essential if we are to profit by the main meaning of *Macbeth*. For the play is so very great that it covers much more than it appears to cover; it will certainly survive our age as it has survived its own; it will certainly leave the twentieth century behind as calmly and completely as it has left the seventeenth century behind. Hence if we ask for the meaning of this classic we must necessarily ask the meaning for our own time. It might have another shade of meaning for another period of time. If, as is possible, there should be a barbaric return and if history is any kind of guide, it will destroy everything else before it destroys great literature. The high and civilized sadness of Virgil was enjoyed literally through the darkest instant of the Dark Ages. Long after a wealthier generation has destroyed Parliament they will retain Shakespeare. Men will enjoy the greatest tragedy of Shakespeare even in the thick of the greatest tragedy of Europe.

It is quite possible that Shakespeare may come to be enjoyed by men far simpler than the men for whom he wrote. Voltaire called him a great savage; we may come to the time far darker than the Dark Ages when he will really be enjoyed by savages. Then the story of Macbeth will be read by a man in the actual position of Macbeth. Then the Thane of Glamis may profit by the disastrous superstitions of the Thane of Cawdor. Then the Thane of Cawdor may really resist the impulse to be King of Scotland. There would be a very simple but a real moral if Macbeth could read *Macbeth*. "Do not listen to evil spirits; do not let your ambition run away with you; do not murder old gentlemen in bed; do not kill other people's wives and children as a part of diplomacy; for if you do these things it is highly probable that you will have a bad time." That is the lesson that Macbeth would have learnt from *Macbeth*; that is the lesson that some barbarians of the future may possibly learn from *Macbeth*. And it is a true lesson. Great work has something to say quite simply to the simple. The barbarians would understand *Macbeth* as a solid warning against vague and violent ambition; and it is such a warning, and they would take along with it this lesson also, which is none the worse because perhaps only the barbarians could adequately understand it. "Distrust those malevolent spirits who speak flatteringly to you. They are not benevolent spirits; if they were they would be more likely to beat you about the head."

Before we talk then of the lesson of a great work of art, let us realize that it has a different lesson for different ages, because it is itself eternal. And let us realize that such a lesson will be in our own day not absolute but suited to the particular vices or particular misfortunes of that day. We are not in any danger at the moment of the positive and concrete actions which correspond to those of *Macbeth*. The good old habit of murdering kings (which was the salvation of so many commonwealths in the past) has fallen into desuetude. The idea of such a play must be for us (and for our sins) more subtle. The idea is more subtle but it is almost inexpressibly great. Let us before reading the play consider if only for a moment what is the main idea of *Macbeth* for modern men.

One great idea on which all tragedy builds is the idea of the continuity of human life. The one thing a man cannot do is exactly what all modern artists and free lovers are always trying to do. He cannot cut his life up into separate sections. The case of the modern claim for freedom in love is the first and most obvious that occurs to the mind; therefore I use it for this purpose of illustration. You cannot have an idyll with Maria and an episode with Jane; there is no such thing as an episode. There is no such thing as an idyll. It is idle to talk about abolishing the tragedy of marriage when you cannot abolish the tragedy of sex. Every flirtation is a marriage; it is a marriage in this frightful sense; that it is irrevocable. I have taken this case of sexual relations as one out of a hundred; but of any case in human life the thing is true. The basis of all tragedy is that man lives a coherent and continuous life. It is only a worm that you can cut in two and leave the severed parts still alive. You can cut a worm up into episodes and they are still living episodes. You can cut a worm up into idylls and they are quite brisk and lively idylls. You can do all this to him precisely because he is a worm. You cannot cut a man up and leave him kicking, precisely because he is a man. We know this because man even in his lowest and darkest manifestation has always this characteristic of physical and psychological unity. His identity continues long enough to see the end of many of his own acts; he cannot be cut off from his past with a hatchet; as he sows so shall he reap.

This then is the basis of all tragedy, this living and perilous continuity which does not exist in the lower creatures. This is the basis of all tragedy, and this is certainly the basis of *Macbeth*. The great ideas of *Macbeth*, uttered in the first few scenes with a tragic energy which has never been equalled perhaps in Shakespeare or out of him, is the idea of the enormous mistake a man makes if he supposes that one decisive act will clear his way. Macbeth's ambition, though selfish and someway sullen, is not in itself criminal or morbid. He wins the title of Glamis in honourable war; he deserves and gets the title of Cawdor; he is rising in the world and has a not ignoble exhilaration in doing so. Suddenly a new ambition is presented to him (of the agency and atmosphere which presents it I shall speak in a moment) and he realizes that nothing lies across his path to the Crown of Scotland except the sleeping body of Duncan. If he does that one cruel thing, he can be infinitely kind and happy.

Here, I say, is the first and most formidable of the great actualities of *Macbeth*. You cannot do a mad thing in order to reach sanity. Macbeth's mad resolve is not a cure even for his own irresolution. He was indecisive before his decision. He is, if possible, more indecisive after he has decided. The crime does not get rid of the problem. Its effect is so bewildering that one may say that the crime does not get rid of the temptation. Make a morbid decision and you will only become more morbid; do a lawlesss thing and you will only

46

get into an atmosphere much more suffocating than that of law. Indeed, it is a mistake to speak of a man as 'breaking out.' The lawless man never breaks out; he breaks in. He smashes a door and finds himself in another room, he smashes a wall and finds himself in a yet smaller one. The more he shatters the more his habitation shrinks. Where he ends you may read in the end of *Macbeth*.

For us moderns, therefore, the first philosophical significance of the play is this; that our life is one thing and that our lawless acts limit us; every time we break a law we make a limitation. In some strange way hidden in the deeps of human psychology, if we build our palace on some unknown wrong it turns very slowly into our prison. Macbeth at the end of the play is not merely a wild beast; he is a caged wild beast. But if this is the thing to be put in a primary position there is something else that demands at least our second one. The second idea in the main story of *Macbeth* is, of course, that of the influence of evil suggestion upon the soul, particularly evil suggestion of a mystical and transcendental kind. In this connection the mystical character of the promptings is not more interesting than the mystical character of the man to whom they are especially sent. Mystical promptings are naturally sweet to a mystic. The character of Macbeth in this regard has been made the matter of a great deal of brilliant and futile discussion. Some critics have represented him as a burly silent soldier because he won battles for his country. Other critics have represented him as a feverish and futile decadent because he makes long practical speeches full of the most elaborate imagery. In the name of commonsense let it be remembered that Shakespeare lived before the time when unsuccessful poets thought it poetical to be decadent and unsuccessful soldiers thought it military to be silent. Men like Sidney and Raleigh and Essex could have fought as well as Macbeth and could have ranted as well as Macbeth. Why should Shakespeare shrink from making a great general talk poetry when half the great generals of his time actually wrote great poetry?

The whole legend, therefore, which some critics have based on the rich rhetoric of *Macbeth*: the legend that Macbeth was a febrile and egotistical coward because he liked the sound of his own voice, may be dismissed as a manifestation of the diseases of later days. Shakespeare meant Macbeth for a fine orator for he made fine speeches; he also meant him for a fine soldier because he made him not only win battles bravely but what is much more to the point, lose battles bravely; he made him, when overwhelmed by enemies in heaven and earth, die the death of a hero. But Macbeth is meant to be among other things an orator and a poet; and it is to Macbeth in this capacity that the evil supernatural appeal is made. If there be any such thing as evil influences coming from beyond the world, they have never been so suggestively indicated as they are here. They appeal, as evil always does, to the existence of a coherent and comprehensible scheme. It is the essence of a nightmare that it turns the whole cosmos against us. Two of their prophecies have been fulfilled; may it not be assumed then that the third will also be fulfilled?

Also they appeal, as evil always does (being slavish itself and believing all men slaves) to the inevitable. They put Macbeth's good fortune before him as if it were not so much a fortune as a fate. In the same way imperialists sought to salve the consciences of Englishmen by giving them the offer of gold and empire with all the gloom of predestination. When the devil, and the witches who are the servants of the devil, wish to make a weak man snatch a crown that does not belong to him, they are too cunning to come to him and say "Will you be King?" They say without further parley, "All hail, Macbeth, that shall be king hereafter". This weakness Macbeth really has; that he is easily attracted by that kind of spiritual fatalism which relieves the human creature of a great part of his responsibility. In this way there is a strange and sinister appropriateness in the way in which the promises of the evil spirits end in new fantasies; end, so to speak, as mere diabolical jokes. Macbeth accepts as a piece of unreasoning fate first his crime and then his crown. It is appropriate that this fate which he has accepted as external and irrational should end in incidents of mere extravagant bathos, in the walking forest and strange birth of Macduff. He has once surrendered himself with a kind of dark and evil faith, to a machinery of destiny that he can neither respect nor understand, and it is the proper sequel of this that the machinery should produce a situation which crushes him as something useless.

Shakespeare does not mean that Macbeth's emotionalism and rich rhetoric prove him to be unmanly in any ordinary sense. But Shakespeare does mean, I think, to suggest that the man, virile in his essential structure, has this weak spot in his artistic temperament; that fear of the mere strength of destiny and of unknown spirits, of their strength as apart from their virtue, which is the only proper significance of the word superstition. No man can be superstitious who loves his God, even if the god be Mumbo-Jumbo. Macbeth has something of this fear and fatalism; and fatalism is exactly the point at which rationalism passes silently into superstition. Macbeth, in short, has any amount of physical courage, he has even a great deal of moral courage. But he lacks what may be called spiritual courage; he lacks a certain freedom and dignity of the human soul in the universe, a freedom and dignity which one of the scriptural writers expresses as the difference between the servants and the sons of God.

But the man Macbeth and his marked but inadequate manliness, can only be expressed in connection with the character of his wife. And the question of Lady Macbeth immediately arouses again the controversies that have surrounded this play. Miss Ellen Terry and Sir Henry Irving

D   49

acted *Macbeth* upon the theory that Macbeth was a feeble and treacherous man and that Lady Macbeth was a frail and clinging woman. A somewhat similar view of Lady Macbeth has been, I believe, consistently uttered by a distinguished American actress. The question as commonly stated, in short, is the question of whether Macbeth was really masculine, and second, of whether Lady Macbeth was not really feminine. The old critics assumed that because Lady Macbeth obviously ruled her husband she must have been a masculine woman. The whole inference of course is false. Masculine women may rule the Borough Council, but they never rule their husbands. The women who rule their husbands are the feminine women and I am entirely in accord with those who think that Lady Macbeth must have been a very feminine woman. But while some critics rightly insist on the feminine character of Lady Macbeth they endeavour to deprive Macbeth of that masculine character which is obviously the corollary of the other. They think Lady Macbeth must be a man because she rules. And on the same idiotic principle they think that Macbeth must be a woman or a coward or a decadent or something odd because he is ruled. The most masculine kind of man always is ruled. As a friend of mine once said, very truly, physical cowards are the only men who are not afraid of women.

The real truth about Macbeth and his wife is somewhat strange but cannot be too strongly stated. Nowhere else in all his wonderful works did Shakespeare describe the real character of the relations of the sexes so sanely, or so satisfactorily as he describes it here. The man and the woman are never more normal than they are in this abnormal and horrible story. *Romeo and Juliet* does not better describe love than this describes marriage. The dispute that goes on between Macbeth and his wife about the murder of Duncan is almost word for word a dispute which goes on at any suburban breakfast-table about something else. It is merely a matter of changing "Infirm of purpose, give me the daggers", into "infirm of purpose, give me the postage stamps". And it is quite a mistake to suppose that the woman is to be called masculine or even in any exclusive sense strong. The strengths of the two partners differ in kind. The woman has more of that strength on the spot which is called industry. The man has more of that strength in reserve which is called laziness.

But the acute truth of this actual relation is much deeper even than that. Lady Macbeth exhibits one queer and astounding kind of magnanimity which is quite peculiar to women. That is, she will take something that her husband dares not do but which she knows he wants to do and she will become more fierce for it than he is. For her, as for all very feminine souls (that is, very strong ones) selfishness is the only thing which is acutely felt as sin; she will commit any crime if she is not committing it only for herself. Her husband thirsts for the crime egotistically and therefore vaguely, darkly, and subconsciously, as a man becomes conscious of the beginnings of physical thirst. But she thirsts for the crime altruistically and therefore clearly and sharply, as a man perceives a public duty to society. She puts the thing in plain words, with an acceptance of extremes. She has that perfect and splendid cynicism of women which is the most terrible thing God has made. I say it without irony and without any undue enjoyment of the slight element of humour.

If you want to know what are the permanent relations of the married man with the married woman you cannot read it anywhere more accurately than in the little domestic idyll of Mr. and Mrs. Macbeth. Of a man so male and a woman so female, I cannot believe anything except that they ultimately save their souls. Macbeth was strong in every masculine sense up to the very last moment; he killed himself in battle. Lady Macbeth was strong in the very female sense which is perhaps a more courageous sense; she killed herself, but not in battle. As I say, I cannot think that souls so strong and so elemental have not retained those permanent possibilities of humility and gratitude which ultimately place the soul in heaven. But wherever they are they are together. For alone among so many of the figures of human fiction, they are actually married.

THE TRAGEDY OF KING LEAR

THE TRAGEDY of *King Lear*, on some of its elements perhaps the very greatest of all the Shakespearian tragedies, is relatively seldom played. It is even possible to have a dark suspicion that it is not universally read; with the usual deplorable result; that it is universally quoted. Perhaps nothing has done so much to weaken the greatest of English achievements, and to leave it open to facile revolt or fatigued reaction, than the abominable habit of quoting Shakespeare without reading Shakespeare. It has encouraged all the pompous theatricality which first created an idolatry and then an iconoclasm; all that florid tradition in which old playgoers and after-dinner speakers talked about the Bard or the Swan of Avon, until it was comparatively easy, at the end of the Victorian era, for somebody like Bernard Shaw to propose an Edwardian massacre of Bards and almost to insinuate that the swan was a goose. Most of the trouble came from what are called 'Familiar Quotations', which were hardly even representative or self-explanatory quotations. In almost all the well-known passages from Shakespeare, to quote the passage is to miss the point. It is almost needless to note what may be called the vulgar examples; as in the case of those who say that Shakespeare asks, "What is in a name?"; which is rather like saying that Shakespeare says murder must be done, and it were best if it were done quickly. The popular inference always is that Shakespeare thought that names do not matter; there being possibly no man on God's earth who was less likely to think so, than the man who made such magnificent mouthfuls out of mandragora and hurricanes, of the names of

Hesperides or Hercules. The remark has no point, except in the purely personal circumstances in which it has poignancy, in the mouth of a girl commanded to hate a man she loves, because of a name that seems to her to have nothing to do with him. The play now under consideration is no exception to this disastrous rule. The old woman who complained that the tragedy of *Hamlet* was so full of quotations would have found almost as many in the tragedy of *King Lear*. And they would have had the same character as those from *Hamlet* or *Romeo and Juliet*: that those who leave out the context really leave out the conception. They have a mysterious power of making the world weary of a few fixed and disconnected words, and yet leaving the world entirely ignorant of the real meaning of those words.

Thus, in the play of *King Lear*, there are certain words which everybody has heard hundreds of times, in connections either intentionally or unintentionally absurd. We have all read or heard of somebody saying, "How sharper than a serpent's tooth it is to have a thankless child." Somehow the very words sound as if they were mouthed by some tipsy actor or silly and senile person in a comic novel. I do not know why these particular words, as words, should be selected for citation. Shakespeare was a casual writer; he was often especially careless about metaphors, careless about making them and careless about mixing them. There is nothing particularly notable about this particular metaphor of the tooth; it might just as well have been a wolf's tooth or a tiger's tooth. The lines quoted only become remarkable when we read them with the rest of the scene, and with a very much more remarkable passage, which is never quoted at all. The whole point of Lear's remark is that, when buffeted by the first insult of Goneril, he breaks forth into a blasting bodily curse upon the woman, praying first that she may have no children, then that she may have horrible and un-natural children, that she may give birth to a monstrosity, *that she may feel how*, etc. Without that terrible implication, the serpent is entirely harmless and his teeth are drawn. I cannot imagine why only the weakest lines in the speech are everlastingly repeated, and the strongest lines in it are never mentioned at all.

A man might well harden into the horrid suspicion that most people have hardly read the play at all, when he remembers how many things there are in it that are not repeated, and yet would certainly be remembered. There are things in it that no man who has read them can ever forget. Amid all the thunders of the storm, it comes like a new clap of thunder, when the thought first crosses the mad king's mind that he must not complain of wind and storm and lightning, because they are not his daughters. "I never gave you kingdoms, called you children." And I imagine that the great imaginative invention of the English, the thing called Nonsense, never rose to such a height and sublimity of unreason and horror, as when the Fool juggles with time and space and tomorrow and yesterday, as he says soberly at the end of his rant: "This prophecy Merlin shall make; for I live before his time." This is one of the Shakespearian shocks or blows that take the breath away. But in the same scene of the storm and the desolate wandering, there is another example of the sort of thing I mean in the matter of quotation. It is not so strong an example, because the words are very beautiful in themselves; and have often been applied beautifully to pathetic human circumstances not unworthy of them. Nevertheless, they are something not only superior, but quite startlingly different, in the circumstances in which they really stand. We have all of us heard a hundred times that some unlucky law-breaker, or more or less pardonable profligate, was "more sinned against than sinning". But the words thus used have not a hundredth part of the point and power of the words as used by Lear. The point of the passage is that he himself challenges the cosmic powers to a complete examination; that he finds in his despair a sort of dizzy detachment of the intellect, and strikes the balance to his own case with a kind of insane impartiality. Regarding the storm that rages round him as a universal rending and uprooting of everything, something that will pluck out the roots of all things, even the darkest and foulest roots of the heart of man deceitful above all things and desperately wicked, he affirms in the face of the most appalling self-knowledge, clear and blasting as the lightning, that his sufferings must still be greater than his sins. It is possibly the most tremendous thing a man ever said; whether or no any man had the right to say it. It would be hard to beat it even in the Book of Job. And it does weaken the particular strength of it that it should be used, however sympathetically, as a cheerful and charitable guess about the weaknesses of other people.

There are certain abstractions very strong in Shakespeare's mind, without which his plays are much misunderstood by modern people, who look to them for nothing whatever except realistic details about individuals. For instance, there runs through the whole play of *King Lear*, as there runs through the whole play of *Richard the Second*, an abstraction which was an actuality of awful vividness to the man of Shakespeare's time; the idea of the King. Under the name of Divine Right, a very unlucky name, it was mixed up with Parliamentary and sectarian quarrels which afterwards altogether dwarfed and diminished its dignity. But Divine Right was originally much more human than that. It resolved itself roughly into this; that there are three forms in which men can accept the idea of justice or the authority of the commonwealth; in the form of an assembly, in the form of a document, or in the form of a man. King Lear is a man; but he is or has been a sacramental or sacred man; and that is why he can be a desecrated man. Even those who prefer to be governed by the scroll of the law, or by the assembly of the tribe, must understand that men have wished, and may again wish, to be governed by a man; and that where this wish has existed the man does become, not indeed divine, but certainly different. It is not an accident that Lear is a king as well as a father, and that Goneril and Regan are not only daughters but traitors. Treason, or what is felt as treason, does break the heart of the world; and it has seldom been so nearly broken as here.

THE EVERLASTING NIGHTS

NO ONE has any business with the *Arabian Nights* who objects to bulk in literature. It is a curious thing which may be noticed by all literary critics, that literature is the only thing in which bulk is considered a defect. The truth is, of course, that size is an element of value in literature. If the quality be really ascertained, the amount, even if indefinitely increased, becomes a merit. A man would as soon think of saying that the field was over-crowded with flowers, that the sky had a surplus population of stars, as of saying that there were too many good stories. The *Arabian Nights* is a collection of extraordinarily good stories, and while the modern aesthetic critic will probably find the book too long, the person with a taste for literature will find it too short. Surely the greatest compliment we can pay to it or any other book is to find it too short. This defect is the highest of all possible perfections.

Now length in the case of the *Arabian Nights* is not a mere material accident; it is one of the essential qualities, one of the essential virtues of the book. A short *Arabian Nights* is as unthinkable as a neat wilderness or a snug cathedral. The whole plan of the book is one vast conspiracy to entrap the reader into a condition of everlasting attention. By a supreme stroke of genius the compiler expressed this in the primary framework and outline. He made the teller of the stories a person inspired to prolong the stories infinitely by the devouring desire of life. It made the wish for an everlasting story one with the wish for an everlasting earthly existence. He made Scheherezade suddenly paralyze the tyrant when

the sword was uplifted by a vision of all the stories that remained to be told in the world. She lured him into the
golden and enchanted chamber of the first story and then the
work was done. He could not get away from the puzzling
and alluring sequence of that chain of tales, that endless
series of delightful mantraps. Rooms within rooms opened
their tempting and tantalizing doors, stories within stories
promised a complicated and even confusing pleasure. The
tyrant can sway kingdoms, and command multitudes, but he
cannot discover exactly what happened to a fabulous prince
or princess unless he asks for it. He has to wait, almost to
fawn upon a wretched slave for the fag-end of an old tale.
Never in any other book, perhaps, has such a splendid tribute
been offered to the pride and omnipotence of art.

This is the real idea behind the *Arabian Nights*. The richness which first strikes the imagination in reading it is a mere
symbol. The richness of gold, silver and jewels is a mere
figure and representation of that which is the essential idea,
the deep and enduring richness of life. The preciousness of
emerald and amethyst and sandal-wood is only the parable
and expression of the preciousness of stones, dust, and dogs
running in the streets. In the *Arabian Nights* everything has a
story to tell. Three men come together; one is leading a
gazelle, another a dog, another a mule. But the gazelle is an
enchanted human being, the dog is a transformed brother,
the mule is a man in unhuman shape. There is no traveller so
dusty and commonplace that he may not have stories to tell
of the terrible continents that lie upon the borderland of the
world. There is no beggar so bent and abject that he may
not have possession of a talisman which gives him power
over the palaces and temples of princes. The possibilities of
life are not to be counted. That is the profoundly practical
moral buried in the *Arabian Nights*.

In our early Biblical lessons we were told that the Eastern
teacher sat down to teach. There are not, perhaps, many

points of resemblance between two such products of Oriental literature as *The Book of Job* and the *Arabian Nights*. But there is this in common between them, that we feel that both must have been narrated by somebody who was sitting down, while Ulysses the typical Greek, was toiling with oar and rudder to discover new isles and peninsulas, Job, the typical Jew, was reviewing the whole of heaven and earth while sitting on a dust-heap. Similarly, the Sultan of the Indies heard the tales of the four quarters of the earth while sitting on a cushion. The essential point, the essential lesson of these Oriental literatures is the clear and most moral lesson of idleness. Idleness is not a vice; in the old Chaucerian form of 'idlesse' it is a pleasure, and almost a virtue. Its true name is leisure. It is not a trifling with unimportant things, but a vision of all the innumerable important things in the universe which are in themselves even more important than bread and cheese.

Here again, therefore, we come near to one of the essential ideas which give their perennial charm to the *Arabian Nights*. It is the idea that idleness is not an empty thing. Idleness can be, and should be a particularly full thing, rich as it is in the *Arabian Nights* with invaluable jewels and incalculable stories. Idleness, or leisure, as the Eastern chronicler would probably prefer to call it, is indeed our opportunity of seeing the vision of all things, our rural audience for hearing, as the Sultan of the Indies heard them, the stories of all created things. In that hour, if we know how to use it, the tree tells its story to us, the stone in the road recites its memoirs, the lamp-post and the paling expatiate on their autobiographies. For as the most hideous nightmare in the world is an empty leisure, so the most enduring pleasure is a full leisure. We can defend ourselves, even on the Day of Judgment, if our work has been useless, with pleas of opportunity, competition and fulness of days.

AESOP'S FABLES

AESOP EMBODIES an epigram not uncommon in human history; his fame is all the more deserved because he never deserved it. The firm foundations of common sense, the shrewd shots of uncommon sense, that characterize all the Fables, belong not to him but to humanity. In the earliest human history, whatever is authentic is universal; and whatever is universal is anonymous. In such cases there is always some central man who had first the trouble of collecting these stories, and afterwards the fame of creating them. He had the fame; and, on the whole, he earned the fame. There must have been something great and human, something of the human future and the human past, in such a man; even if he only used it to rob the past or deceive the future. The story of Arthur may have been really connected with the most fighting Christianity of falling Rome or with the most heathen traditions hidden in the hills of Wales. But the word 'Mappe' or 'Malory' will always mean King Arthur; even though we find older and better origins than the Mabinogian; or write later and worse versions than the 'Idylls of the King.' The nursery fairy-tales may have come out of Asia with the Indo-European race, now fortunately extinct; they may have been invented by some fine French lady or gentlemen like Perrault: they may possibly even be what they profess to be. But we shall always call the best selection of such tales, 'Grimm's Tales'; simply because it is the best collection.

The historical Aesop, in so far as he was historical, would seem to have been a Phrygian slave, or at least one not to be specially and symbolically adorned with the Phrygian cap of liberty. He lived, if he did live, about the sixth century before Christ, in the time of that Croesus whose story we love and suspect like everything else in Herodotus. There are also stories of deformity of feature and a ready ribaldry of tongue; stories which (as the celebrated Cardinal said) explain, though they do not excuse, his having been hurled over a high precipice at Delphi. It is for those who read the Fables to judge whether he was really thrown over the cliff for being ugly and offensive, or rather for being highly moral and correct. But there is no kind of doubt that the general legend of him may justly rank him with a race too easily forgotten in our modern comparisons; the race of the great philosophic slaves. Aesop may have been a fiction like Uncle Remus; he was also, like Uncle Remus, a fact. It is a fact that slaves in the old world could be worshipped like Aesop, or loved like Uncle Remus. It is odd to note that both the great slaves told their best stories about beasts and birds.

But whatever be fairly due to Aesop, the human tradition called Fables is not due to him. This had gone on long before any sarcastic freedman from Phrygia had or had not been flung off a precipice; this has remained long after. It is to our advantage, indeed, to realize the distinction; because it makes Aesop more obviously effective than any other fabulist. Grimm's Tales, glorious as they are, were collected by two German students; at least we know more about them than we know about a Phrygian slave. The truth is, of course, that *Aesop's Fables* are not Aesop's fables, any more than *Grimm's Fairy-Tales* were ever Grimm's fairy-tales. But the fable and the fairy-tale are things utterly distinct. There are many elements of difference; but the plainest is plain enough. There can be no good fable with human beings in it. There can be no good fairy-tale without them.

Aesop, or Babrius (or whatever his name was), understood that, for a fable, all the persons must be impersonal. They must be like abstractions in algebra, or like pieces in chess. The lion must always be stronger than the wolf, just as four is always double of two. The fox in a fable must move crooked, as the knight in chess must move crooked. The sheep in a fable must march on, as the pawn in chess must march on. The fable must not allow for the crooked captures of the pawn; it must not allow for what Balzac called "the revolt of a sheep." The fairy-tale, on the other hand, absolutely revolves on the pivot of human personality. If no hero were there to fight the dragons, we should not even know that they were dragons. If no adventurer were cast on the undiscovered island – it would remain undiscovered. If the miller's third son does not find the enchanted garden where the seven princesses stand white and frozen – why then, they will remain white and frozen and enchanted. If there is no personal prince to find the Sleeping Beauty she will simply sleep. Fables repose upon quite the opposite idea: that everything is itself, and will in any case speak for itself. The wolf will be always selfish; the fox will be always foxy. Something of the same sort may have been meant by the animal worship, in which Egyptian and Indian and many other great people have combined. Men do not, I think, love beetles or cats or crocodiles with a wholly personal love; they salute them as expressions of that abstract and anonymous energy in nature which to any one is awful, and to an atheist must be frightful. So in all the fables that are or are not Aesop's all the animal forces drive like inanimate forces, like great rivers or growing trees. It is the limit and the loss of all such things that they cannot be anything but themselves; it is their tragedy that they could not lose their souls.

This is the immortal justification of the Fable; that we could not teach the plainest truths so simply without turning men into chessmen. We cannot talk of such simple things without using animals that do not talk at all. Suppose, for a moment, that you turn the wolf into a selfish baron, or the fox into a foxy diplomatist, you will at once remember that even barons are human, you will be unable to forget that even diplomatists are men. You will always be looking for that accidental good humour that should go with the brutality of any brutal man; for that allowance for all delicate things, including virtue, that should exist in any good diplomatist. Once put a thing on two legs instead of four and pluck it of feathers and you cannot help asking for a human being, either heroic, as in the fairy-tales, or unheroic, as in the modern novels.

But by using animals in this austere and arbitrary style as they are used on the shields of heraldry or the hieroglyphics of the ancients, men have really succeeded in handing down those tremendous truths that are called truisms. If the chivalric lion be red and rampant, it is rigidly red and rampant; if the sacred ibis stands anywhere on one leg, it stands on one leg for ever. In this language, like a large animal alphabet, are written some of the first philosophic certainties of men. As the child learns A for Ass or B for Bull or C for Cow, so man has learnt here to connect the simpler and stronger creatures with the simpler and stronger truths. That a flowing stream cannot befoul its own fountain, and that any one who says it does is a tyrant and a liar; that a mouse is too weak to fight a lion, but too strong for the cords that can hold a lion; that a fox who gets most out of a flat dish may easily get least out of a deep dish; that the crow whom the gods forbid to sing, the gods nevertheless provide with cheese; that when the goat insults from a mountain-top it is not the goat that insults, but the mountain; all these are deep truths deeply graven on the rocks wherever men have passed. It matters nothing how old they are, or how new; they are the alphabet of humanity, which like so many forms of primitive picture-writing employs any living symbol in preference to man. These ancient and universal tales are all of animals; as the latest discoveries in the oldest prehistoric caverns are all of animals. Man, in his simpler stories, always felt that he himself was something too mysterious to be drawn. But the legend he carved under these cruder symbols was everywhere the same; and whether fables began with Aesop or began with Adam, whether they were German and medieval as Reynard the Fox, or as French and Renaissance as La Fontaine, the upshot is everywhere essentially the same; that pride goes before a fall; and that there is such a thing as being too clever by half. You will not find any other legend but this written upon the rocks by any hand of man. There is every type and time of fable; but there is only one moral to the fable; because there is only one moral to everything.

BOTH SIDES OF THE LOOKING-GLASS

We all say comparisons are odious, and I wonder whether any of us know why. In the abstract, comparison is only a way of testing degrees and qualities, like the zoologist who thought it an exact and exhaustive description of a giraffe to say that "he is taller than an elephant, but not so thick". There is nothing in this to indicate any odium – to suggest that he was cruel to wild elephants or unduly spoiled and petted his giraffes. But when we pass from nature to human nature, comparison does always sound like a depreciation. I think the reason is this: that for some cause, possibly original sin, we have a very weak supply of words of praise as compared with our rich and varied output of terms of abuse. We can call the unpleasant scholar or intellectual a pedant or a prig, but we have no special word for the pleasant sort of scholar or intellectual. We can call the wrong sort of society person a snob, but we have no special name for the right sort of society person. Thus we are driven to the ghastly necessity, for instance, of calling our friends 'nice'. Fancy calling Dr. Johnson 'nice', and Fox 'nice', and Nelson 'nice'. It does not present very vivid or varied portraits.

I have been reading, side by side, two books about men who were both 'nice', and whose books were 'nice'. They were the two great nineteenth-century tellers of tales to children. They were also as flatly contrary to each other at every point as two men could be, but if I go beyond calling them both 'nice' and try to compare them or say what they were like, it will quite certainly sound as though I were praising one and blaming the other. This is simply because we cannot vary praise as we vary blame. One of these men was Charles Dodgson, commonly known as Lewis Carroll, a don at Oxford and a very Victorian English clergyman, the other was Hans Christian Andersen, a queer, cranky and visionary Danish peasant, and the author of immortal tales.

When I say that Lewis Carroll was very Victorian, that will sound like a reproach, though it ought to be a compliment as well as a reproach – only it is so much more difficult to find words to fit what was good in Victorian England than what was bad in it. If I say that Dodgson the don was conventional or comfortable or respectable, compared with Andersen the peasant, those words will sound like unfriendly words, but only because there are no friendly words to express the really friendly things that often do go along with conventions and comforts.

It is abominably stupid to call the Victorian Age merely conventional and comfortable, and to forget the fact that it produced a new kind of poetry which was supremely wild and supremely innocent. It was the poetry of pure nonsense, which has never been known in the world before and may never be known again. Lewis Carroll was not the only example: Edward Lear, I think, was a better one; and I would put in a word for the 'Katawampus' and other stories of Judge Parry, that children loved at least as much. Lewis Carroll's letters to children prove that not only did he love children, but that children loved him; nevertheless I believe his intellectual attacks were directed to adults. Everything in Lewis Carroll is part of what he called the Game of Logic; it is very Victorian, by the way, to think of logic as a game. The Victorians had to invent a sort of impossible paradise in which to indulge in good logic: for all serious things they preferred bad logic. This is not paradoxical, or at any rate, it was they who made the paradox. Macaulay and Bagehot

THE SPICE OF LIFE

and all their teachers taught them that the British Constitution ought to be illogical – they called it being practical. Read the great Reform Bill and then read *Alice in Wonderland* – you will be struck by the resemblance of *Alice in Wonderland*. They had to go to fairyland to be logical. Thus I suspect that the very best of Lewis Carroll was not written by a man for children, but by a don for dons. The most brilliant strokes are not only mathematical, but mature. Ten lectures against the heresy of mere Relativity could be based on that one perfect sentence, "I have seen hills compared with which that would be a valley."

But it may be questioned whether the little girls he wrote for were tortured by relativist scepticism. And, in a way, this is part of the glory of Lewis Carroll. He was not only teaching children to stand on their heads; but he was also teaching dons to stand on their heads. It is a good test of a head to stand on it. When the Victorians wanted a holiday, they made one, a real intellectual holiday. They did create a world which, to me at least, is still a sort of strange home, a secret holiday, a world in which monsters, terrifying in other fairy-tales, were turned into pets. Nothing will deprive them of the glory of it. It was nonsense for nonsense's sake. If we ask where this magic mirror was found the answer is that it was found among very padded Victorian furniture: in other words, it was due to the historical accident by which Dodgson and Oxford and England were, at that moment, very comfortable and secure. They knew there would be no fighting, except the party system, in which Tweedledum and Tweedledee agreed to have a battle, the battle being much less obvious than the agreement. They knew their England could not see invasion or revolution; they knew it was growing richer by commerce; they did not realize that agriculture was dying, possibly because it was already dead; they had no peasants.

They found their flat contrary in that other great lover of

children, whose story is told admirably in *The Life of Hans Christian Andersen* by Signe Toksvig. Hans Andersen was himself a peasant, and came of what is still a country of peasants. In a thousand ways, Hans Andersen represented the exact opposite of the sheltered don in his cushioned Victorian drawing-room. Hans was open to all the winds that blew, like a peasant on his fields, like a peasant on the European battlefields. He grew up anyhow, full of a sort of pathetic and greedy ambition, such as dons at Oxford do not show. He had experienced all realities, including his own weakness and his own desires. He did a hundred things, idiotic things, which Mr. Dodgson would have found unthinkable; but because he was a peasant he had his compensations. He remained in touch with the enormous tradition of the earth in the matter of mystery and glamour – he did not have to make a new and rather artificial sort of fairy-tale out of triangles and syllogisms.

Hans Andersen was not only an uncle loved by children, he was a child. He was one of those great children of our Christian past who have had the Divine favour which is called arrested development. His faults were the faults of a child – and very annoying faults they were. Why do aged men after reading this book, love Hans Andersen? I answer, because the most lovable thing in the world is humility. Now Hans Andersen had a vast vanity, which was founded on humility. I know that modern psychologists have called the combination an inferiority complex – but there is always an element of humility in the man who does not conceal his vanity.

Nobody ever made it so naked and shameless as poor Hans Andersen. But my intention here is only to stir such thoughts as are aroused by those contrasted types, neither of which, I hope, will ever be forgotten as nursery classics. Both had many imitators, I hope I shall not be misunderstood if I say that Hans Andersen was perhaps even greater, because he was himself an imitator. That great peasant, that great poet in prose, had the peasant quality which the Victorians had lost – the old mystical feeling about the ordinary materials of life. Hans Andersen would have found more on this side of the looking-glass than Alice found on the other. Beyond are fantastic mathematical projections; but why go through the looking-glass when all the rest of the furniture, all the chairs and tables, can be animated by elves?

My comparisons are becoming odious. It is because there is no variation in verbal praise. Differentation sounds like depreciation. Which is better; to have distilled from the dense commercial solidity of the modern world a wild new wine or honey of intellectual nonsense, or to have enlarged that large and magnificent accumulation of popular imagination in the past, and to have made again, with an original note, the great fairy-tale that is really a folk-tale? I only know that if you try to deprive me of either of them, there will be a row.

AND SO TO BED

I WILL not say that the Englishman is the most subtle of all
the beasts of the field; for he is obviously not a beast, still
less a snake, and least of all a devil. But it is true that he is in
many ways the most complex type in Christendom. He is
never so complex as when he is not entirely conscious; and
especially when the last twist of his labyrinthine complexity
takes the form of claiming to be simple; to be rough and
tough and bluff like Major Bagstock. And one of the weirdest
things about him is the subconscious or semi-conscious
art and skill, with which he arranges history and human
facts so as to soothe and satisfy himself, without quite clearly
realising what he is doing or why he is doing it. In truth, the
Englishman is the one man really made for psycho-analysis.
He really does instinctively erect screens and scenery, half
symbolic and half secretive, to protect a hidden thought. All
these things filtered through my mind in reading Mr. Arthur
Bryant's excellent last volume on Pepys: *Samuel Pepys: The
Years of Peril.*

Nine men out of ten in this country, above the most un-
lettered class, could tell you with some confidence who Pepys
was. He was a funny fellow who kept a Diary. He was a
roguish fellow, and the fun of his Diary consists chiefly in his
confessions of infidelity to a wife, or flirtations with a cham-
bermaid. He wrote in quaint short sentences, often parodied
in the newspapers; and he ended as many entries as possible
with the phrase, "and so to bed". Now it is a very queer
thing that this should be so universally known, and that
nothing else about the same man should be known at all.

71

For this mildly scandalous journal was only kept for a short time, comparatively early in his life; and even so the proportion of scandal is exaggerated. There were not many men in England then, or possibly now, whose sincere confessions in youth would be very different. Meanwhile, the rest of his life was a public life of practical usefulness and profound importance. He, with about one other man, made modern England a great naval power. The reply, it will be generally supposed, is that the public heard of the Diary first, long ago, while curious scholars have lately dug up the details about the permanent official. But in mere common sense, the case is exactly the other way. The Diary was kept in a close cipher, apparently impenetrable and long unpenetrated. But the political life of Pepys had been no more private than the public life of Cromwell or Cardinal Wolsey. Political foes tried to impeach him as openly as Warren Hastings in Westminster Hall; that he might be executed as openly as Charles I at Whitehall. In the famous phrase of the Regicide, this thing was not done in a corner. His foes were the first men of the age, like Shaftesbury and Halifax; and they filled the streets with mobs of the Brisk Boys with the Green Ribbons, roaring for the blood of such servants of the Crown. And the roguish little fellow of the Diary stood up under that storm and steered like a ship the policy that has launched the ships of England. He fought for a fighting fleet, more or less of the modern model, exactly as Cobden fought for Free Trade or Gladstone for Home Rule. And he did not write anything corresponding to "and so to bed" till he had seen those ships make their harbour. Now why is that most exciting passage in patriotic history practically left out of our rather too patriotic histories? Why is the hero of it known only as a buffoon winking at a maidservant? There is no reason that can be called simple, in the sense of superficial. Pepys was a very normal national man; Protestant like any other and as insular as most. Englishmen, especially English historians, are excessively devoted to what is national and very particularly to what is novel. And it is hardly exaggerative to say he could have written "Samuel Pepys", like the signature of a craftsman or architect, under the word *Victory* where it shone upon the ship of Nelson.

There is only one explanation. There can be no other; and it is simply this. You cannot praise the patriotism of Pepys without also praising the patriotism of James II, then James, Duke of York. You cannot tell the story at all, without letting it stand out with startling clearness that Samuel Pepys the Protestant might never have started work, and would certainly never have done the work, without the devoted practical support, and even prompting, of James Stuart the Papist. And *his* story had to be told so as to enforce only one moral; that Papistry was the enemy of Patriotism. In plain words, you have to admit that the prince, who did more than any other to enable Britannia to rule the waves, was the same Prince who was driven across the same waves into exile, simply and solely because he was a Roman Catholic. And that was more than the English historians dared to admit; merely to do justice to the patriotism of a poor little Government official. That single catastrophe, in the way of letting the Catholic cat out of the Protestant bag, would have turned upside-down the whole orthodox official academic History of England.

But the point is, as I have said, that the thing is almost unthinkably subtle, often semi-conscious; and at once collective and secretive. It is a sort of vague but repeated gesture (like that of somebody stroking the cat) which has gradually put all this lively part of history to sleep; and moulded the story so as to soothe the successful side. There is no veto on studying the period; no overt official command to take a certain line; there was simply an instinct to take the line of least resistance. The main facts of the time were seldom even contradicted; they were only neglected. And I can imagine

73

with what a stare of simple wonder I should be regarded, by the man in the street, who is quite willing to talk to me about Pepys, if I said there was a sort of conspiracy to connect Pepys only with his Diary. Is not the Diary a very amusing book? Yes. Was not Pepys a Protestant? Yes. Do we not generally praise patriots, especially Protestant patriots? Yes. But if Pitt or Palmerston or Disraeli had written a very amusing Diary, people would discuss each statesman with reference to his statesmanship; and then say, "I always think he is most delightful in his Diary. Have you read his Diary?"

By this vast vague corporate craft or silent strategy, there has been built up in this country a quite abnormal condition of mental and moral Comfort. And we know, because Mr. Winston Churchill tells us in the *Strand Magazine*, that we have a noble Parliament and more freedom than any foreigners; and a poor man has as much chance as a rich man in our courts of law. And so to bed.

AS LARGE AS LIFE IN DICKENS

NOTHING IS more characteristic of Dickens, nothing has
so handicapped him with the languid modern reader as the
vast crowding of his stage with innumerable and bewilder-
ingly well-painted characters. He has passed through a period
in which it has been customary among certain people to de-
ride him; but the whole indifference to Dickens has arisen
from the strange idea that literature should copy life. While
realism was in full swing it was easy to point out that no person ever existed so horrible as Quilp, or so grandiloquent as
Snodgrass, or unscrupulous as Ralph Nickleby, so entirely
pathetic as Little Nell. But we have tired of realism. We have
suddenly awakened to the fact that art has nothing to do
with copying. It is strange, but true, that the same movement
and discovery which has been the justification of Aubrey
Beardsley has been the justification of Dickens.

Dickens, of course, has been a great deal handicapped
by the common habit among his admirers of praising him for
the wrong things. He is praised for being 'true to life', while
his true merit is not that he is true to life, but alive. It is common to hear a man say when Dickens is accused of exaggeration, "I have met a man exactly like Pecksniff." Of
course, to begin with, he has not met a person like Pecksniff
any more than he has met one like Caliban. And further, if
he had met a man exactly like Pecksniff, it would go far to
show that Dickens was not a great novelist. Since no two men
in real life are exactly like each other, so no fictitious character ought to be exactly like a real character. He ought to
be an addition to the existing stock of real characters. His

passions and traditions, his instincts and memories, should be blended together in entirely new quantities into an entirely new colour never seen before from the beginning upon the palette of life. If it be true (as I believe it is) that no person precisely like Mrs. Micawber ever existed or ever will exist in the whole domain of the universe, then we know that Mrs. Micawber is like life. We know that Dickens created as Life itself creates.

This is the far higher sense in which great art is 'like life', far higher, that is, than the ordinary sense in which the phrase is used. Great literature is like life. Not because it is accurate to the leaves on the tree and the pattern on the carpet and the words men actually employ; it is like life because it has in it the exuberant energy of life, its power of production, its sense of hope and memory, its consciousness of an almost immortal vitality. Great literature, in short, is like life because it also is living. An admirer of Dickens, therefore, ought to be ashamed of defending the great master by pretending that he did not exaggerate. He exaggerated by the same living law which makes the birds chatter in pairing time or the kitten fight with its own tail. The passion behind all his work was joy, and the final touch of exaggeration is the absolute necessity of the great literature of joy.

This mistake about Dickens arose, of course, because a critical generation had forgotten altogether that there even was such a thing as the great literature of joy. We have fallen into the way of thinking that literature is a refuge for weak temperaments, that literature may express all the darker and quainter moods, all the moods of regret or rebellion or hesitation, but never that one universal mood, streaming like a river through heaven and earth, by which alone all things consent to live. Dickens has seemed to us vulgar and impossible, and sprawlingly inartistic, for the simple reason that he is too strong for us. His bewildering crowds and mobs of characters, his vast mazy travels over

England and America, his endless banquets and conversations, his intense realism and his frantic unreality, are all manifestations of a quite insatiable and omnivorous power of mental pleasure to which our period has lost the key. He was the last of the great comic writers; since his time we have lost the power of realizing the connection between the words 'great' and 'comic'. We have forgotten that Aristophanes and Rabelais stand with Aeschylus and Dante; that their folly was wiser and more solid than our wisdom, and that their levity has outlasted a hundred philosophies. Dickens exaggerates, and it is not a fault but a merit; it is of the same kind as the exaggerations of the great French humorist, whose vigorous and almost monstrous power of happiness was only contented with a giant who could lift his head above Notre Dame and ride away with the bells upon his bridle. Therefore Dickens has become to the orthodox artistic world of today what Rabelais has become to many of the modern schools – a thing obscure with excess of jesting, a positive darkness of joy.

There are many evidences that the great truth and passion behind the work of Dickens was this sense of joy in things; just as much as the great truth and passion behind Thackeray was a sense of their almost sacred pathos, or the great truth and passion behind Hawthorne a sense of their weird significance. But the best evidence of all lies in the fact that Dickens was never so triumphantly successful as in describing the type of man whose existence in this world, in which he has neither money nor honour, seems to depend entirely on his high spirits and his capacity for realizing the magnificence of the flying moment. All Dickens' sticks of heroes and dolls of heroines may, of course, be thrown aside: the real ideal figure of Dickens is William Micawber. Dick Swiveller, his next best character, is a man of the same type; they both represent a kind of shabby poet, whose continual lack of money and utter antagonism to the order of society can never kill him, because of his everlasting pleasure in old memories and very old quotations. They have alike the same mutability, the same impecuniosity, the same florid, but genuine, taste in literature, the same continual and crushing misfortunes, the same mysterious, but unbreakable, immortality. They are never ended, because, fools and rascals as they are they hold on to something which belongs, not to society but to the soul: the power of joy. And note here that Dickens, in describing these men who are nearest to his heart, is not only vigorous, living and entertaining, as he always is, but far truer to the facts even than is his wont. Pecksniff is a spirited and amusing bogey for a pure farce, but such a hypocrite never lived in this mean earth; we shall meet him in a better and bolder world. Mr. Squeers is a good, black grotesque figure from the outside, but he has no inside. But Micawber and Swiveller (especially the latter) are true to the tenor of life; they see the humour of their own exaggerations, they live avowedly on their own good spirits. And in them Dickens really touches problems and elements of greatness which are as old as the world and as great as any tragedy. He touches, for example, the great tragedy of Ireland, which, after innumerable sorrows still lives upon an outrageous gaiety. Above all he touches the case of the great masses of the poor, whom he loved. He saw deeper than a hundred statisticians and philanthropic economists. No man on earth was ever a more fierce and mutinous Radical than he; but he saw that all calculations of the mortal hours of men left out the everlasting moment.

DISPUTES ON DICKENS

AN INTERESTING little controversy began some time ago in the *Academy* on the position of Dickens, and it throws a flood of light on the real character of the temporary reaction against that great novelist's fame. 'E.A.B.', the able and decisive *Academy* critic is a typical representative of the school devoted to 'Art' in its more technical sense, and like all the critics of that school he has a clear, hard and almost scientific critical method of critical test. Dickens falls in his eyes because of what he calls his 'artistic ignorance and indifference' and his lack of 'feeling for literature', all of which means that Dickens was not an artist of the particular pattern which French fiction in the nineteenth century has made essential and even popular.

Of course, this particular scheme of criticism will say what it has to say and pass, as so many other schemes of criticism have passed. We shall never, thank Heaven, have a sound and conclusive scheme of literary art, any more than we shall have a scheme of theology which makes the universe as obvious as a figure in geometry. If there were produced a really final and satisfactory justification of religion on logical grounds, most healthy-minded people would immediately cease to believe in religion; and if there were such a justification of art, most healthy-minded people would cease to believe in art. Touching these high matters we can endure anything except that they should turn out to be so small that we can even understand them. And so the 'Art for Art's Sake' school of criticism will be found to be merely relative and in a century or so Flaubert the critic will be as dead and

79

as interesting as Aristotle. But Flaubert the novelist will remain impeccable and also Dickens the novelist. For it is only the things which are deliberately built to last for ever which cannot do so.

The real reason of the temporary eclipse of the fame of Dickens is not that he was a faulty artist but that he expressed almost faultlessly a certain class of thoughts and emotions which happen at this moment to be almost absent from the cultivated class. It was not that he expressed badly but that we know nothing at all about the kind of thought and sentiment that he expressed well. It was not that he had a deficiency in his art, it is we that have a deficiency in our experience. The work of Dickens appears to us rambling and shapeless for precisely the same reason that the work of Maeterlinck would have appeared to Dickens rambling and shapeless. There is a mood at the back of the whole work of Dickens as much as there is a mood at the back of the whole work of Maeterlinck; and it must be confessed with shame, as far as I am concerned, that our mood is the mood of Maeterlinck and not the mood of Dickens. To 'E.A.B.' and his school, 'Pickwick' is not exactly either good or bad; it is simply not a novel at all. To the very best critics of Dickens' time, 'Pelleas and Melisande' would have been something not exactly good or bad but simply not a drama at all. If they had seen it acted they would not have thought that the drama was deteriorating. They would only have thought that they themselves were going mad.

The truth is that whole schools of art and of great art can become merely mysterious and imbecile to the most enlightened generations if those generations do not cultivate the particular emotions by which those schools of art are inspired. Thus, for example, the whole of the Italian art, from Giotto to Botticelli would have appeared and did appear to the critics of the eighteenth century an ugly and infantile exhibition like the scrawlings of a child upon a slate. To the

eighteenth century it was quite obvious that these medieval
pictures were mere despicable beginnings. Their lines were
drawn wrong, their colours were arranged wrong, their
figures were anatomical monstrosities, their landscapes had
the absurdity of Noah's Ark, their saints had the grimness of
an army of idiots. No blasphemer had ever dared to draw
upon his darkest page a picture so impious as this picture of an
insane universe with its grinning angels, its gaping saints. Not
the most secret volume of eighteenth-century atheism had conceived in its wrath and satire such a celestial parody as these
painters had conceived in their humility and faith. Such was
the impression which Christian art produced on the whole of
the 'age des philosophes': that it was an example of an almost
shocking innocence like a baby's picture of God.

Then came the nineteenth century when man felt again
the same emotions which had been felt in the time of Giotto.
Men of the boldest and most liberal intellects began to dream
the great medieval dream of a united and devout Christendom. Men of the ripest taste and opinion began to join
celibate brotherhoods and school themselves with fast and
flagellation. Poets, painters and musicians went back to the
splendid superstitions of medieval Europe, and collected tales
and delusions as industriously as a scientist could collect facts.
Upon the whole nation descended again the great mood of
mystery, the nameless convictions, the certainties that have
no origin and the hopes that have no end. And with a start
of indescribable surprise men found themselves looking at
those dark old Italian pictures with new eyes. The lines that
went wrong now went right; they perfectly expressed a quaint
and delicate severity. The landscapes that looked absurd now
looked enchanted; they were lit with the morning of the
world. The faces that had been hideous had grown beautiful
like the face of a good man when we have come to know him
and cannot imagine any other features being the perfect
picture of his soul. This is what has happened again and

again in the world and will continue to happen until the end. When a set of emotions are unfamiliar to a people, the art which expresses them will appear not only superstitious but obviously inartistic. When a set of emotions become familiar to a people, the art which expresses them will appear not only philosophical but obviously artistic.

People who do not share the sentiment of Maeterlinck do not say that he is not moral or true to life, they say he does not write plays. People who do not share the sentiment of Whitman do not say that he is not right or not worthy, they say that he does not write poetry. People who do not share the sentiment of Dickens do not say that he is too optimistic or too conventional, they say that he had "absolutely no feeling for literature".

When we come to examine the case of Dickens carefully, we find that this is exactly what has happened. The characteristics which 'E.A.B.' and other critics note as the defects of Dickens are in a great many instances the proper and inevitable modes of expressing a certain gigantic conviviality and cordiality. For example, 'E.A.B.' speaks of the formlessness of 'Pickwick', but he does not notice that what he calls formlessness was in fact a well-known and celebrated artistic form among the elder and more convivial writers. The sprawling and seemingly disconnected novel of comic adventure was a recognized and excellent form of art. Recent criticism I believe is accustomed to describe it as the 'picaresque' novel. For when we come to think of it, the whole point is very simple. The new impressionist method of brevity, restraint, and an adhesion to one central image or incident is the right and proper literary form to express the kind of things which the new Impressionist novel wishes to express; the little ironies, the sad small stories that end without an ending; the faces that are too bitter for tears. About these sort of things it may be said, not as a commonplace phrase, but as a sound and telling rule of art, that the less said about them the better. One flash of literary lightning revealing a woman dead in a garret with a victorious army marching by is enough if the sentiment concerned is the sentiment of a pitiful irony. But it is not enough if the sentiment is that of the ancient camaraderies and immortal enterprises of the 'picaresque' novel.

You cannot exhibit Sam Weller in a flash of lightning. The whole emotional significance of Sam Weller depends upon the idea that like some warrior of the mythic ages, he has passed unscathed through infinite adventures and will pass unscathed through innumerable adventures. The reason of the whole matter is that of misfortune we all desire to say little and that the words in a French short story should be few, like the words in a house of mourning. But the moment we come into the atmosphere of positive delight and exultation a new element enters in, the desire to linger. Books like 'Pickwick' are the most lingering. Men linger over their walks, over their talks, over their stories, over their dinners. All the characters seem friends who are talking together far into an immortal night to which no grey morning ever comes.

The formlessness of 'Pickwick' is therefore its form. This mood of exuberance has two natural expressions, the desire to linger and the desire to ramble. If Pickwick and his friends were not continually crossing a crowded stage which was for ever changing like a transformation scene and of which they only were the constant factors, it would not be a better book but a worse. If the whole story revolved round one incident like a story by Guy de Maupassant, if everything turned on the Fancy Dress Ball at Eatonswill or the Cricket Match at Dingley Dell, if the central symbol of the whole story were Mr. Sawyer's red handkerchief or Mr. Winkle's horse; if the *Pickwick Papers* in short were only a brilliant fragment of psychology about the fat boy, or a sad sea-green little idyll about Mr. Stiggins, it would not be a better book but a worse, for it would have lost its supreme meaning even as we have lost its sense of a world almost choked with adventure and a hero constant only in the mutability of a comic Ulysses, faithful only to his own omnivorous fickleness.

CHARLOTTE BRONTË AS A
ROMANTIC

THE GENIUS of Charlotte Brontë is unique in the only valuable sense in which the word can be applied; the only sense which separates the rarity of some gift in a poet from the rarity of some delusion in an ayslum. However complex or even grotesque an artistic power may be, it must be as these qualities exist in a key, which is one of the most complex and grotesque of human objects, but which has for its object the opening of doors and the entrance into wider things. Charlotte Brontë's art was something more or less than complex; and it was not to be described as grotesque; except rarely – and unintentionally, But it was temperamental and, like all things depending on temperament, unequal; and it was so personal as to be perverse. It is in connection with power of this kind, however creative, that we have to discover and define what distinguished it from the uncreative intensity of the insane. I cannot understand what it was that made the Philistines of a former generation regard *Jane Eyre* as morally unsound; probably it was its almost exaggerated morality. But if they had regarded it as mentally unsound, I could have understood their prejudice, while perceiving the nature of their error.

Jane Eyre is, among other things, one of the finest detective stories in the world; and for any one artistically attuned to that rather electric atmosphere, the discovery of the mad wife of Rochester is, as that type of sensation should always be, at once startling and suitable. But a stolid reader, trained in a tamer school of fiction, might be excused if he came to the conclusion that the wife was not very much madder than her husband, and that even the governess herself was a little queer. Such a critic, however, would be ill-taught, as people often are in tame schools; for the mildest school is anything but the most moral. The distinction between the liberating violence that belongs to virtue, as distinct from the merely burrowing and self-burying violence that belongs to vice, is something that can only be conveyed by metaphors; such as that I have used about the key. Some may feel disposed to say that the Brontë spirit was not so much a key as a battering-ram. She had indeed some command of both instruments, and could use the more domestic one quietly enough at times; but the vital point is that they opened the doors. Or it might be said that Jane Eyre and the mad woman lived in the same dark and rambling house of mystery, but for the maniac all doors opened continually inwards, while for the heroine all doors, one after the other, opened outwards towards the sun.

One of these universal values in the case of Charlotte Brontë is the light she throws on a very fashionable aesthetic fallacy: the over-iterated contrast between realism and romance. They are spoken of as if they were two alternative types of art, and sometimes even as if they were two antagonistic directions of spiritual obligation. But in truth they are things in two different categories; and, like all such things, can exist together, or apart, or in any degree of combination. Romance is a spirit; and as for realism, it is a convention. To say that some literary work is realistic, not romantic, is to be as inconsequent as the man who said to me once, "The Irish are warm-hearted, not logical." He, at any rate, was not logical, or he would have seen that his statement was like saying that somebody was red-haired rather than athletic.

There is no reason why a man with strong reasoning power should not have strong affections; and it is my experience, if anything, that the man who can argue clearly in the abstract generally does have a generosity of blood and instincts. But he may not have it, for the things are in different categories. This case of an error about the Irish has some application to the individual case of Charlotte Brontë, who was Irish by blood, and in a sense, all the more Irish for being brought up in Yorkshire. An Irish friend of mine, who suffers the same exile in the same environment, once made to me the suggestive remark that the towering and over-masculine barbarians and lunatics who dominate the Brontë novels, simply represent the impression produced by the rather boastful Yorkshire manners upon the more civilized and sensitive Irish temperament. But the wider application is that romance is an atmosphere, as distinct as a separate dimension, which co-exists with and penetrates the whole work of Charlotte Brontë; and is equally present in all her considerable triumphs of realism, and in her even greater triumphs of unreality.

Realism is a convention, as I have said; it is generally a matter of external artistic form, when it is not a matter of mere fashion or convenience, how far the details of life are given, or how far they are the details of the life we know best. It may be rather more difficult to describe a winged horse than a war horse; but after all it is as easy to count feathers as to count hairs; it is as easy and as dull. The story about a hero in which the hairs of his horse were all numbered would not be a story at all; the line must be drawn a long while before we come to anything like literal reality; and the question of whether we give the horse his wings, or even trouble to mention his colour, is merely a question of the artistic form we have chosen. It is the question between casting a horse in bronze or carving him in marble; not the question of describing a horse for the purposes of a zoologist or for the purposes of a bookie. But the spirit of the work

is quite another thing. Works of the wildest fantasticality in form can be filled with a rationalistic and even
a sober spirit; as are some works of Lucian, of Swift and
of Voltaire. On the other hand, descriptions of the most
humdrum environments, told with the most homely in-
timacy, can be shot through and through with the richest intensity, not only of the spirit of sentiment but of the spirit of
adventure.

Few will be impelled to call the household of Mr. Rochester
a humdrum environment, but it is none the less true that
Charlotte Brontë can fill the quietest rooms and corners
with a psychological romance which is rather a matter of
temperature than of time or place. After all, the sympathetic
treatment of Mr. Rochester in *Jane Eyre* is not more intrinsically romantic and even exaggerative than the sympathetic
treatment of Mr. Paul Emanuel in *Villette*; though the first
may be superficially a sort of demon and the second more
in the nature of an imp. To present Mr. Emanuel sympathetically at all was something of an arduous and chivalric
adventure. And Charlotte Brontë was chivalric in this perfectly serious sense; perhaps in too serious a sense, for she
paid for the red-hot reality of her romance in a certain in-
sufficiency of humour. She was adventurous, but in an intensely individualistic and therefore an intensely womanly
way.

It is the most feminine thing about her that we can think
of her as a knight-errant, but hardly as one of an order or
round table of knights-errant. Thackeray said that she reminded him of Joan of Arc. But it is one of the fascinating
elements in the long romance of Christendom that figures like
Joan of Arc have an existence in reality. This vision of the
solitary virgin, adventurous and in arms, is very old in
European literature and mythology; and the spirit of it went
with the little governess along the roads to the dark mansion
of madness as if to the castle of an ogre. The same rule had

run like a silver thread through the purple tapestries of Ariosto; and we may willingly salute in our great country-woman, especially amid the greatest epic of our country, something of that nobility which is in the very name of Britomart.

ANTI-RELIGIOUS THOUGHT IN THE EIGHTEENTH CENTURY

THE ECLIPSE of Christian theology during the rationalist advance of the eighteenth century is one of the most interesting of historical episodes. In order to see it clearly, we must first realize that it was an episode and that it is now historical. It may be stating it too strongly to say that it is now dead; it is perhaps enough to say that it is now distant and yet distinct; that it is divided from our own time as much as any period of the past. Neither reason nor faith will ever die; for men would die if deprived of either. The wildest mystic uses his reason at some stage; if it be only by reasoning against reason. The most incisive sceptic has dogmas of his own; though when he is a very incisive sceptic, he has often forgotten what they are. Faith and reason are in this sense co-eternal; but as the words are popularly used, as loose labels for particular periods, the one is now almost as remote as the other. What was called the Age of Reason has vanished as completely as what are called the Ages of Faith.

It is essential to see this fact first, because if we do not see its limitations we do not see its outline. It has nothing to do with which period we prefer, or even which we think right. A rationalist is quite entitled to look back to the eighteenth century as a golden age of good sense, as the medievalist looks back to the thirteenth century as a golden age of good faith. But he must look back, and look back across an abyss. We may like or dislike the atmosphere of the modern world, with its intense interest in anything that is called psychological, and in much that is called psychical. We may think that speculation has gone more deep or that it has grown more morbid. We may like or dislike the religions of faith-healing or spirit-rapping; or a hundred other manifestations of the same mood, in fields quite remote from the supernatural or even the spiritual. We may like or dislike, for instance, that vast modern belief in "the power of suggestion" expressed in advertising or publicity and educational methods of all sorts. We may like or dislike the appeal to the non-rational element; the perpetual talk about the Sub-conscious Mind or the Race Memory or the Herd Instinct. We may deplore or we may admire all these developments. But we must fix it in our minds as a historical fact that to any one of the great 'Infidels' or Freethinkers of the eighteenth century, this whole modern world of ours would seem a mere madhouse. He might almost be driven, in pursuit of the reasonable, to take refuge in a monastery.

We are dealing therefore with an episode and even an interlude; though the man who likes it has as much right to say that it was an hour of happy daylight between the storms as a Christian has to say it of primitive Christianity or medieval Christendom. From about the time that Dryden died a Catholic to about the time that Newman began to write a little less like a Protestant, there was a period during which the spirit of philosophy filling men's minds was not positively Protestant any more than it was positively Catholic. It was rationalist even in Protestants and Catholics; in a Catholic like Pope or a Protestant like Paley. But it can be seen at the clearest when the last clinging traditions or pretences were dropped; when the most stolid specimen of the Protestant middle classes is found busily scribbling sneers in the footnotes and even the index of a great history of the Fall of Rome; when a brilliant pupil going forth out of the Jesuit seminary turns back over his shoulder the terrible face of Voltaire.

In order to exhibit the essential quality, let us first compare the period with that which preceded it. Touching its historical causes, no man with a sense of human complexity will offer anything but contributory causes. But I think there are contributory causes that have been strangely overlooked. On the face of it, it refers back to the Renaissance, which refers back to the old pagan world. On the face of it, it also refers back to the Reformation, though chiefly in its negative aspect or branch in the old Christian world. But both these things are connected with a third, that has not, I think, been adequately realized. And that is a feeling which can only be called futility. It arose out of the disproportion between the dangers and agonies of the religious wars and the really unreasonable compromise in which they ended; *cujus regio ejus religio*: which may be translated, "Let every State establish its State Church", but which did mean in the Renaissance epoch, "Let the Prince do what he likes."

The seventeenth century ended with a note of interrogation. Pope, the poet of reason, whom some thought too reasonable to be poetical, was once compared to a question mark, because he was a crooked little thing that asked questions. The seventeenth century was not little, but it was in some ways crooked, in the sense of crabbed. But anyhow it began with the ferocious controversies of the Puritans and it ended with a question. It was an open question, but it was also an open wound. It was not only that the end of the seventeenth century was of all epochs the most inconclusive. It was also, it must be remembered, inconclusive upon a point which people had always hoped to see concluded. To use the literal sense of the word 'conclude', they expected the wound to close. We naturally tend to miss this point today. We have had nearly four hundred years of divided Christianity and have grown used to it; and it is the Reunion of Christendom that we think of as the extraordinary event. But they still thought the Disunion of Christendom an extraordinary event. Neither side had ever really expected it to remain in a state of Disunion. All their traditions for a thousand years were of some sort of union coming out of controversy, ever since a united religion had spread all over a united Roman Empire. From a Protestant standpoint, the natural thing was for Protestantism to conquer Europe as Christianity had conquered Europe. In that case the success of the counter-Reformation would be only the last leap of a dying flame like the last stand of Julian the Apostate. From a Catholic standpoint the natural thing was for Catholicism to reconquer Europe, as it had more than once reconquered Europe; in that case the Protestant would be like the Albigensians: a passing element ultimately reabsorbed. But neither of these natural things happened. Prussia and the other Protestant principalities fought against Austria as the heir of the Holy Roman Empire in the Thirty Years War. They fought each other to a standstill. It was utterly and obviously hopeless to make Austria Protestant or Prussia Roman Catholic. And from the moment when that fact was realized the nature of the whole world was changed. The rock had been cloven and would not close up again, and in the crack or chasm a new sort of strange and prickly weed began to grow. The open wound festered.

We have all heard it said that the Renaissance was produced or precipitated by the Fall of Constantinople. It is true in a sense perhaps more subtle than is meant. It was not merely that it let loose the scholars from the Byzantine Court. It was also that it let loose the sceptical thoughts of the scholars, and of a good many other people when they saw this last turn of the tide in the interminable strife between Christ and Mahomet. The war between Islam and Christendom had been inconclusive. The war between the Reformation and the counter-Reformation was inconclusive. And I for one fancy that the former fact had a good deal to do with the full sceptical expansion of the eighteenth century. When men saw the Crescent and the Cross tossed up alternately as a juggler tosses balls, it was difficult for many not to think that one might be about as good or bad as the other when they saw the Protestant and the Catholic go up and down on the see-saw of the Thirty Years War. Many were disposed to suspect that it was six to one and half-a-dozen to the other. This addition involved an immense subtraction; and two religions came to much less than one. Many began to think that, as they could not both be true, they might both be false. When that thought had crossed the mind the reign of the rationalist had begun.

The thought, as an individual thought, had of course begun long before. It is, in fact, as old as the world; and it is quite obviously as old as the Renaissance. In that sense the father of the modern world is Montaigne; that detached and distinguished intelligence which, as Stevenson said, saw that men would soon find as much to quarrel with in the Bible as they had in the Church. Erasmus and Rabelais and even Cervantes had their part; but in these giants there was still a great gusto of subconscious conviction, still Christian; they mocked at the lives of men, but not at the life of man. But Montaigne was something more revolutionary than a revolutionist; he was a relativist. He would have told Cervantes that his knight was not far wrong in thinking puppets were men, since men are really puppets. He would have said that windmills were as much giants as anything else; and that giants would be dwarfs if set beside taller giants. This doubt, some would say this poison in its original purity, did begin to work under the surface of society from the time of Montaigne onwards and worked more and more towards the surface as the war of religions grew more and more inconclusive. There went with it a spirit that may truly be called humane. But we must always remember that even its refreshing humanity had a negative as well as a positive side. When people are no longer in the mood to be heroic, after all, it is only human to be humane. Some men were really tolerant, but others were merely tired. When people are tired of the subject, they generally agree to differ.

But against this clear mood, as against a quiet evening sky, there stood up the stark and dreadful outlines of the old dogmatic and militant institutions. Institutions are machines; they go on working under any sky and against any mood. And the clue to the next phase is the revolt against their revolting incongruity. The engines of war, the engines of torture, that had belonged to the violent crises of the old creeds, remained rigid and repellent; all the more mysterious for being old and sometimes even all the more hideous for being idle. Men in that mellow mood of doubt had no way of understanding the fanaticism and the martyrdom of their fathers. They knew nothing of medieval history or of what a united Christendon had once meant to men. They were like children horrified at the sight of a battlefield.

Take the determining example of the Spanish Inquisition. The Spanish Inquisition was Spy Fever. It produced the sort of horrors such fevers produce; to some extent even in modern wars. The Spaniards had reconquered Spain from Islam with a glowing endurance and defiance as great as any virtue ever shown by man; but they had the darker side of such warfare; they were always struggling to deracinate a Jewish plot which they believed to be always selling them to the enemy. Of this dark tale of perverted patriotism the humanitarians knew nothing. All they knew was that the Inquisition was still going on. And suddenly the great Voltaire rose up and shattered it with a hammer of savage laughter. It may seem strange to compare Voltaire to a child. But it is true that though he was right in hating and destroying it, he never knew what it was that he had destroyed.

There was born in that hour a certain spirit, which the Christian spirit should be large enough to cover and understand. In relation to many things it was healthy, though in

95

relation to some things it was shallow. We may be allowed to associate it with the jolly uncle who does not believe in ghosts. It had an honourable expression in the squires and parsons who put down the persecution of witches. The uncle is not always just to Spiritualists; but he is rather a comfort on a dark night. The squire did not know all there is to know about diabolism, but he did stop many diabolical fears of diabolism. And if we are to understand history, that is humanity, we must sympathize with this breezy interlude in which it seemed natural for humanity to be humane.

The mention of the squire is not irrelevant; there was in that humanity something of unconscious aristocracy. One of the respects in which the rational epoch was immeasurably superior to our own was in the radiant patience with which it would follow a train of thought. But it is only fair to say that in this logic there was something of leisure, and indeed we must not forget how much of the first rational reform of the age came from above. It was a time of despots who were also deists or even, like Frederick the Great, practically atheists. But Frederick was sometimes humanitarian if he was never human. Joseph of Austria, offending his people by renouncing religious persecution, was very like a squire offending the village by repressing witch-burning. But in considering the virtues of the age, we must not forget that it had a very fine ideal of honourable poverty; the Stoic idea of Jefferson and Robespierre. It also believed in hard work, and worked very hard in the details of reform. A man like Bentham toiled with ceaseless tenacity in attacking abuse after abuse. But people hardly realized that his utilitarianism was creating the new troubles of Capitalism, any more than that Frederick of Prussia was making the problem of modern militarism.

Perhaps the perfect moment of every mortal thing is short, even of mortal things dealing with immortal, as was the best moment of the Early Church or the Middle Ages. Anyhow the best moment of rationalism was very short. Things always overlap, and Bentham and Jefferson inherited from something that had already passed its prime. Not for long did man remain in that state of really sane and sunny negation. For instance, having covered the period with the great name of Voltaire, I may well be expected to add the name of Rousseau. But even in passing from one name to the other, we feel a fine shade of change which is not mere progression. The rationalist movement is tinged with the romantic movement, which is to lead men back as well as forward. They are asked to believe in the General Will, that is the soul of the people; a mystery. By the time the French Revolution is passed, it is elemental that things are loose that have not been rationalized. Danton has said, "It is treason to the people to take away the dream". Napoleon has been crowned, like Charlemagne, by a Pope. And when the dregs of Diderot's bitterness were reached; when they dragged the Goddess of Reason in triumph through Notre Dame, the smouldering Gothic images could look down on that orgy more serenely then than when Voltaire began to write; awaiting their hour. The age was ended when these men thought it was beginning. Their own mystical maenad frenzy was enough to prove it: the goddess of Reason was dead.

One word may be added, to link up the age with many other ages. It will be noted that it is *not* true, as many suppose, that the rational attack on Christianity came from the modern discoveries in material science. It had already come, in a sense it had already come and gone, before these discoveries really began. They were pursued persistently partly through a tradition that already existed. But men were not rationalistic because they were scientists. Rather they became scientists because they were rationalists. Here as everywhere the soul of man went first, even when it denied itself.

THE CAMP AND THE CATHEDRAL

IT MUST always be something of a problem how far the private amateur may venture merely to guess that the professional specialist is mistaken. On the other hand it is quite certain that the man who knows most about a thing is often quite wrong about it. He is often quite wrong in fact, and still more wrong in spirit. On the other hand, the fact that the learned man has lost humility is no reason why the unlearned man also should lose that humorous and healthy gift. On the whole, I think the test of the question is in the size and simplicity of the mistake. It depends on whether the scholar is blind to something because it is too small to be seen, or because it is too large to be seen. I cannot draw the learned man's attention to something recondite, for he knows far more of such obscure details than I do. But I may sometimes draw his attention to something obvious, for that is the sort of thing that the learned man has a way of falling over in the street.

History is the only hobby in which I have dabbled even in this tentative fashion; and it is to history that I should specially apply the test. I mean the test of whether the truth has been missed because it is small and hidden, or actually because it is big and plain. Cobbett, for instance, was an amateur historian in somewhat the same sense, though less amateurish than myself. And when he was right, as I think he generally was, it was because he had an eye for large and obvious things. His eye went across a great landscape like a bird, and was master of the lie of the land. Thus his broadest deduction was simply from the big churches in England,

and especially from the very fact of their bigness. It was a fact filling the sky; a thing whose shadow lay at evening on the whole landscape. But it never seems to have occurred to anybody but Cobbett at that time, to ask whether a sparse remnant of ignorant savages were likely to have raised a sort of sacred tower of Babel to the stars, in half the hamlets of England.

The obscurantism of the Reformation, and the rationalists who were its heirs, was in this way quite unique. Nobody before or since ever kept a people quite so much in darkness as those who put out all the candles in the sixteenth century. In this, for instance, the anti-Catholic reaction in the sixteenth century was quite different from the first Catholic movement in the fourth or fifth century. The Early Christians had a great moral horror of the last phase of the great civilization of Rome; but they never attempted to pretend that it was not a great civilization, or that it had not been made by Rome. Their moral horror was in most matters justified; in some matters considerably exaggerated. But in its wildest exaggerations of fanaticism, it never talks as if the heathen had not built bridges or produced poetry. They did not call the classical architecture the Vandal architecture, as if it had been built only by the barbarians who destroyed it. Yet that would have been a parallel to the very word 'Gothic' which we are still compelled by custom to use. The medieval world did not talk about Plato and Cicero as fools occupied with futilities; yet that is exactly how a more modern world talked of the philosophy of Aquinas and sometimes even of the purely philosophic parts of Dante. The Christians recognized an awful spiritual chasm dividing them from their great ancestors; but they recognized that their ancestors were great. At no moment in all those two thousand years was the legend lost that Virgil was something magnificent, whether as a magician in the Dark Ages or a model classic in the Middle Ages. In religion and morals

99

there had indeed been a shuddering recoil; but it was a recoil from over-civilization, not a complacent contempt for
savagery. They thought the Coliseum had been the arena of
bestial abominations; of beasts, employed by men in a spirit
too base to be called beastly; and so it had. But they did not
think the Coliseum had been made by beasts; or look at its
labyrinth of arches with contemptuous curiosity, as at the
rude instinctive architecture of an ant-hill. In all that mixture
of regret and pain and fascination, with which paganism has
haunted the Christian centuries, there was never a touch of
the innocent vulgarity with which even the Victorians sometimes talked of monks as if they were monkeys.

Now the lifting of this load of obscurantism was a thing
largely done by the light of nature, by men like William
Cobbett or William Morris. And the light of nature showed
them very simple and solid things like the large churches in
the English countrysides. These things are the unanswerable
arguments of the amateur. These are the big guns that he
can really bring up in order to outflank the specialist. Con-
stitutional historians like Hume and Hallam and Robertson
might have read many things that the adventurous amateur
could not read, but it was impossible to pretend that he
could not have access to his own huge empty parish church.
It required no spectacles to see a church spire; and the stones
of Winchester needed no interpreter to translate them from
the Latin. These facts were soon found sufficient, to anyone
who would use his senses; and it became more and more self-
evident that men had been about some very big business in
medieval times. The researches of later and more learned
scholars confirmed the random commonsense of Cobbett or
Morris. But ignorant men had originally made the right
guess; and made it merely because they refused to explain
away a mountain, or ignore the presence of a whale.

I have remarked that nobody ever tried to do with
Roman remains what was once done with Gothic remains. I

mean the attempt to treat them not merely as ruins but as rudiments. I mean the attempt to look at the stone arches as we look at stone hatchets, or regard carved pillars as we regard chipped flints. Nobody ever condescended to heathen architecture, as they condescended to Christian architecture. As a matter of fact it is far more impossible for us to build a Gothic abbey than a Roman aqueduct. The engineering work of the pagan empire does in many ways resemble the works of more modern times. It resembles them largely because the method is scientific. It resembles them still more because the labour is servile. You could build a Roman aqueduct and improve on a Roman aqueduct with scientific appliances. But you cannot build a Gothic cathedral with servile labour. People who want to work in that way must put up with the Pyramids and the Eiffel Tower. And this brings me to a final consideration, in this matter of Roman and medieval remains, which has often intrigued and attracted me as an amateur in historical guesswork. It is a yet larger though somewhat looser application of the same principle, that the things that are hid from the wise and understanding are the things that are too large for them to see.

I have often wondered whether the vastness and vitality of the legends that descend from the Dark Ages, such as the legends of King Arthur and the Round Table, were due to this comparative continuity between the last strength of the Empire and the first strength of the Church. I mean that there may have been a moment, even in Britain, when that majesty of the old pagan civilization still stood unchanged, save that it was no longer pagan. The combination of the old pride in being Roman with the new pride in being Christian may have created a militant morality really not unlike its later form of medieval chivalry. In other words, the popular tradition may not be so far wrong when it talks of some dim fighter in the fifth century as a knight. It may not be so far wrong when it talks of the table where those fighters feasted as the original model of knighthood. It is only by a sort of symbol that we clothe the body of that British king in thirteenth century armour; but it may be something more than a symbol which clothes his spirit with the thirteenth century conception of arms. If ever history did repeat itself, the mood of the first Crusaders who fought with the Saracens might really very well have repeated, as in a mirror, the mood of the last baptized Romans and Romanized Britons who fought with the Saxons. It is really a historical fallacy to say that the courtliness and polish of Sir Lancelot would not have existed in that barbarous time. Courtliness and polish are exactly the things that would have existed in one of the last of the Romanized Christians in comparison with his barbarous time. It is a blunder to say that the virginity and the vision of Sir Galahad are a later romantic fiction added to a half-heathen struggle. Virginity and visions are exactly the ideas that would have shone among the last champions of a Catholic culture in a half-heathen struggle. In this matter of Arthurian legend, I am disposed to suspect that the romantic view is really the realistic view, and the right view. If others doubt it, it will not be because of any realistic arguments of history against it. It will be because others do not feel as I do the enormous argument from the scale of popular stories; the sense that a story we have all heard from childhood is something solid and colossal, like a Gothic cathedral or a Roman camp.

THE RELIGIOUS ASPECT OF
WESTMINSTER ABBEY

EVERY NOW and again in the long and weary history of
literature and journalism something is said that is important,
something that blows a trumpet and calls a halt. For the first
time, perhaps for many years we have suddenly to stop and
think. There remains the essential difference between a
sentence that is read once and a sentence that is read twice.
Now, one of these arresting and transfiguring hints can be
found in Hilaire Belloc's *The Historic Thames*. He says it was
a mere accident of history that the phrase Westminster Abbey
does not sound to us today like the phrase Welbeck Abbey. It
would give the modern English a great shock if Westminster
Abbey were turned into a suite of rooms for the Duke of
Westminster. Yet it gives them no shock that Welbeck Abbey
should be turned into a suite of rooms for the Duke of Port-
land. Yet God was worshipped, I suppose, in Welbeck Abbey
as well as in Westminster Abbey. The first fact about Westminster Abbey, considered as a religious institution, is as
simple as it is sardonic. It is the great religious institution of
the Middle Ages that managed to survive.

The whole of this theme is, of course, subject to exaggeration on both sides. One of the ablest men I have ever known
summed up all the tombs at Westminster which tourists go to
see in the curt and confident formula: "Westminster Abbey
is to be venerated, not because of those that sleep therein, but
rather in spite of them." Many may call this a harsh paradox;
but if they walk round the Abbey seriously and slowly, and
really observe what petty politicians and third-rate generals

have cumbered the ground there with their cold and clumsy monuments, I do not think that they will wholly deny the truth of that idle but bitter jest. A very great part of the funereal art in the Abbey can really be expressed only by one of those colossal epigrams which can be found in the Gospels more than anywhere else. It is, indeed, such statuary as would be made by the dead burying their dead.

It is true that anyone knowing the savour either of England or Christianity will have the religious emotion as well as the patriotic by the low Gothic tomb of Chaucer. But this, if it be examined, is an exception that proves the rule. For Chaucer was buried there when the popular Christianity of the Middle Ages still coloured this church like all others. It would be appropriate in any case that Chaucer should be in Westminster Abbey, even if it were exactly what it was when he used to look out of his London window at its towers. But it would be far more appropriate if men like Pitt or Macaulay were buried in St. Paul's Cathedral; the new Renaissance St. Paul's, which seems built as a pantheon for the heathen but heroic aristocrats of the seventeenth and eighteenth centuries. Florid pillars and posturing statues are appropriate to them; most of them died rather defying death than looking for immortality. And it is really a part of their patriotic, but not Christian spirit that their figures should, as it were, stand frozen for ever in some gesture of eloquence or pride. No imaginative person will wholly fail to respond to the emotion expressed about a murdered Renaissance prince by a great English Renaissance poet:

> He is there
> Up like a Roman statue and will stand
> Till dawn has made him marble.

But to Chaucer all this would have been utterly incomprehensible in connection with a church. In that connection he would have thought it as insolent and vulgar as a waxwork show. For he lived before the great lords had become the legend of England, instead of the great saints. Chaucer, whatever his own faults or vanities might be, would certainly have been the first to admit that it was the Abbey that sanctified his dust and not his dust that sanctified the Abbey. He would not have thought of it as a gallery or public record office where the names and deeds of great poets could be found, though it is likely enough that he knew he was a great poet, and even, among his worldly acquaintances, warmly insisted on the fact. He would have thought of the Abbey as a refuge, where a poor old sinner named Geoffrey Chaucer might feel a little more comfortable in the *Dies Irae*. I am not here choosing by ethical preference between the two attitudes; still less do I despise either one or the other. The name of Nelson, for instance, will always be not only an inspiring but, properly understood, a purifying name. And it seems quite appropriate for Nelson, in his own time, type, station and tradition, to cry out, "A peerage or Westminster Abbey!" meaning by Westminster Abbey merely glory and death. But I doubt if Chaucer could have been made to understand what a peerage could possibly have to do with Westminster Abbey. Warriors at least as valiant and victorious as Nelson were buried in Chaucer's day – the Black Prince, for instance. Warriors at least as valiant and victorious as Nelson were buried at Westminster in the Middle Ages – Henry V, for instance. But when their images were carved on their tombs at all they were carved with closed eyes and hands pointed in prayer. And I have seen one such monument, in Salisbury Cathedral, I think, in which the man lies in dumb supplication, but the dog at his feet has risen erect and watchful, having heard the trumpet of God. It has nothing to do with men being religious men in the modern sense, or even with their being good men. It is a matter of a great popular religion which never affects anybody except when it affects everybody. King John would have been quite incapable of imagining himself exhibited in a church in any other attitude.

I am not here discussing, of course, anything about the ecclesiastical changes as they affect theology; still less should I dream of saying that the spirit Chaucer would have understood did not continue at all in the Anglican Church after the spoliation of the monasteries. It continued markedly in George Herbert, and most unmistakably in Bishop Ken. But all that is a controversy with which, fortunately, we are not here concerned. My point for the moment is purely political; I say that the rise of England into a great modern nation, the particular kind of aristocracy that ruled it while it rose; the greater severance for various reasons from the other European nations, and everything that culminated in the victorious war against Napoleon and the established peace of Queen Victoria – I say that all this did, in fact, produce a type of public spirit and public art in which the old religious significance of the Abbey sometimes almost disappeared. The idea increased that Westminster Abbey was a pantheon, more sensible, but no less secular, than the absurd Valhalla that the Kaiser had at Berlin, where some petty Teuton prince was represented as a giant and Goethe put beside him as a pigmy. That singular mixture of humour and shame which is the English temperament, saved us from doing anything so bad as that. Our statues, at the worst, were only conspicuous by being bad statues, like the old statue of the Duke of Wellington. At the best, they are conspicuous by not being there at all, like the new statue of Shakespeare. But there was enough of this parade of pompous sculpture to confuse or hide the spiritual meaning of Westminster Abbey, and sometimes even its architectural style. We talk of not being able to see the wood for the trees. It may be said that people cannot in this case see the church for the tombs.

All that the Abbey meant to the ethics and atmosphere of this island from its earliest foundations is a thing not easy to state to the average modern reader. For the average modern reader, however well educated, is always taught the tale of the early Middle Ages in such a way that it makes no sense. This is because the main concern of the Middle Ages was the same as the main concern of this article; and it is almost always entirely left out. To take one working instance at random, the ordinary schoolboy of a good school, such as the school I went to, is always told, and therefore naturally believes, that Richard Coeur de Lion was a romantic and irresponsible ne'er-do-well who went away to the Crusades for the same reason that an adventurer takes the King's shilling or a schoolboy runs away to sea – an itch for fighting or an impatience of honest work. Now, whatever Richard's temperament may have been (and, no doubt, it was adventurous) this explanation simply does not cover the facts. Especially it does not cover these two facts – that John, who stopped to rule, was quite as fond of fighting as Richard, and did it very well; and that Philip Augustus of France, who went on the Crusade with Richard, was not particularly fond of fighting, and would very much have liked to stop and rule. The key that is lost here is simply a little thing called the Christian religion, in which all these men, good and bad, believed, and which was in a mortal peril from which the Christian peoples simply expected their Kings to defend it. Now, we could find a somewhat similar instance of the religious element being missed, and the whole business being therefore unmeaning, in the earlier history of Westminster Abbey. The usual way of writing in England about the times before and after the Norman Conquest is to represent it at best as what Carlyle called a "rude stalwart age"; an age of crowned freebooters, who neither asked nor gave mercy; an age of race conquering race with a sort of savage fair play and a more or less useful settlement; in short, a time when instincts laid a foundation on which ethics had yet to build. Anyone taking this ordinary heathen and dynastic view of the business would see something very fierce and final in the coincidence which Freeman maintained, that the Saxon Harold was crowned in Westminster Abbey almost immediately before he was killed at Hastings, and that the victorious Duke of Normandy was certainly crowned in Westminster Abbey almost immediately afterwards. The blood and iron theory of the Dark Ages would see in this the overwhelming of a race by a race; the soft, unguarded Saxons with their soft, unguarded King, Edward the Confessor, swept to nowhere by a raid of aliens clad in iron, appealing to nothing but force, and caring nothing for England. But the person holding this theory would instantly be pulled up short, and extremely puzzled by the discovery that the next really important thing that happened in Westminster Abbey after the Normans were in full possession of it was the canonization of Edward the Confessor. Stated in the modern manner, his difficulty would stand something like this: What made a number of William's own Norman bishops, French gentlemen like any other, join in glorifying the memory of an old fool who had failed to save the Saxons from the victorious arms of their own uncles and cousins? Why should mere strong men, mere victors, bow down to the very weakest man of the defeated party and the subject race? Here, again, the key is always left out; the real explanation is never given. It will be found in the title of this article.

It was based, in short, on one broad and simple fact, which will seem almost incredible to people living in an age when religion is generally the product of a specially religious temperament. The fact was, to put it shortly, that though William the Conqueror had taken Edward the Confessor's land, he did, in all probability, really regard Edward the Confessor as his superior. These fighting men of the Dark Ages were very fierce; but they did really think, ideally speaking, that it would be better if they were very gentle.

They were all soldiers; they would all have agreed that soldiers were inferior to saints. If we say of the men in the ages during which the Abbey was first erected, that they did not curb their coarse and cruel appetites, that in so far as they were tyrants and usurpers they went on being tyrants and usurpers, we shall probably be right. But if we read into them a modern philosophy of force, and imagine that they despised monks or despised meekness, we shall be exactly as wrong as if we supposed that all City men despise a soldier for having been fool enough to have gone under fire. Christianity was to these men exactly what patriotism is to modern Englishmen; the one sacred bond which even the most evil men would not like to own they had betrayed.

This fact of the old and real religious sentiment about the Abbey can be illustrated by any one out of the ten or twenty most famous things in it. Take the case of two celebrated men of the later Middle Ages, a father and a son, who were perhaps as responsible as anyone for the last turn taken by the medieval civilization in England, and who are both more or less connected with the place. I mean Henry IV, called Bolingbroke, and his son, the victor of Agincourt. There is nobody who has heard of Westminster Abbey who has not heard of the Jerusalem Chamber. There may even be few who have heard of the Jerusalem Chamber who have not been told by some guide-book or cicerone that Henry of Bolingbroke died there. But I think there are very much fewer people who would instantly remember (though the fact is known, of course, to all students of such things) that this very selfish, cynical and materialistic usurper found a strange spiritual comfort in dying in the Jerusalem Chamber, because it seemed to him a half fulfilment of a vow which had haunted his life, a vow to die or recover Jerusalem. The sentiment, in fact, was almost exactly the same as had moved a much more heroic man in a much more heroic medieval period, King Robert Bruce, to send his best warrior out of a much-menaced country, to carry his heart to the Holy Land, since he himself had never managed to carry there his powerful body and his powerful brain. To such men Westminster Abbey was not a national and finally satisfying thing. To such men Westminster Abbey was even a *pis aller*. When we have understood that, we have some glimpse of that burning concentration of the Christian conscience which made the Christendom of the Middle Ages almost one nation. But when modern humanitarians talk of international solidarity and the need for a United States of Europe, I do not notice that they give much praise to the Popes and the Crusades who so nearly made it a reality.

The case of Henry V carries me back to an instance of which I am not so sure, and of which I have not the details by me. But I am certain that I read in some quarter of competent learning and authority that Henry V's entry into Paris was marked by proceedings which would very much astonish any good modern English poet, if he were called upon to write a patriotic poem on the event. To do these modern men of genius justice, I think it would have considerably surprised Shakespeare himself, for though Shakespeare was unquestionably in sympathy with the medieval type of religion in such vital matters as the admission or the purgation of sin, the note of international and European Christianity had been somewhat lost even by his time. In the account I read, so far as I remember, the principal interest displayed by Henry V entering Paris after Agincourt was a strong desire to pay homage to the various relics of celebrated saints which were preserved in that city. So that the conqueror of France, though in many ways a rather exceptionally rude and ruthless conqueror may almost be said to have passed a considerable part of his triumphal progress on his knees. These are the things (and I could give twenty other instances with more certainty and exactitude than I can give this one) which really strike the note of the extraordinary and universal conviction of medieval men, and exactly what the men who really made the Abbey would have meant by its religious aspect.

I am not writing controversially and I do not desire in this place to diminish the credit of the Imperial type of patriotism, but in the matter of spiritual atmospheres it is not untrue to say that if Chaucer or even Sackville, had read Mr. Kipling's poetry and understood it they would simply not have been able to make head or tail of what he meant when he said:

> The hush of the dread high altar
> Where the Abbey makes us We.

They would not have been able to understand how a vague Darwinian like Cecil Rhodes, who called a lonely hill in Africa "his church", could have anything to do with the Abbey at all. It is not necessary to take so extreme a view in order to see that the two alternative courses which the religion of Western Europe may take are in a certain sense symbolized in the position of the Abbey today. At this moment the secular and the religious aspects of the institution are still more or less balanced. But under the searching light of spiritual tragedies, which more and more divide the nations into the friends and the enemies of the old proclamation of Constantine, the institution will almost certainly become more of one thing or more of the other. Our religion will either become more and more what the religion of the old Roman poets and historians so largely became, a certain savour of sanctity clinging round the emblems of patriotism and civic pride, so that the tattered flags above the altar will be at last more sacred than the altar itself. Or it will become more and more what that mysterious energy was before which the Roman religion of the poets and the historians perished – a voice out of the catacombs and a cry from the Cross.

THE RELIGIOUS AIM OF EDUCATION

IT IS only by a definite and even deliberate narrowing of the mind that we can keep religion out of education. I do not deny that it may in certain cases be the least of many evils; that it may be a sort of loyalty to a political compromise; that it is certainly better than a political injustice. But secular education is a limitation, if it be only a self-limitation. The natural thing is to say what you think about nature; and especially, so to speak, about the nature of nature. The first and most obvious thing that a person is interested in is what sort of world he is living in; and why he is living in it. If you do not know, of course, you will not be able to say; but the mere fact of not being able to answer the question that the other person is most likely to ask, may or may not be what some people call education, but it is not a very brilliant exhibition of instruction. If you have convictions upon these cosmic and fundamental things, whether negative or positive, you are an instructor who is on one most important point refusing to instruct. Your motive may be generous, or it may be merely timid; but certainly it is not in itself educational.

It is sometimes said that the devotees of a doctrinal religion, who are so often depicted as donkeys, are in matters of this kind wearing blinkers. The word is not wisely chosen by the critics; and in one sense is much more applicable to the critic himself. The man who teaches authoritative answers to ultimate questions, even if he only says that Mumbo Jumbo made the world out of a pumpkin, may be dogmatizing or

persecuting or tyrannically laying down the law about everything, but he is not blinking anything. He is not wearing
blinkers, which implies deliberately limiting the field of his
own vision. His vision may be in our view an illusion; but
if it is very vivid to him, we cannot blame him for describing
it; and anyhow he is describing the whole of it. If there is
such a thing in the world as a donkey deliberately wearing
blinkers, it is the enlightened educationist who is always
making a nervous effort to keep out of his task of imparting
knowledge any reference to the things that men from the
beginning of the world have most wanted to know. Nor are
those things mere hole-and-corner objects of a special
curiosity. Whether or no they can ever be known, they are
not only worth knowing, but they are the simplest and most
elementary sort of knowledge. It is a good thing that children
should fully realize that there is an objective world outside
them, as solid as the lamp-post out in the street. But even
when we make the lamp-post quite objective, it is not un-
natural to ask what is its object. A naturalist, noting the
common objects of the street, may observe many facts and
put them down in a note-book. A bicyclist may bump into a
lamp-post; a tramp may lean against a lamp-post; a drunkard may embrace a lamp-post or even in a lighter moment
try to climb a lamp-post. But it is not a strange or specialist
sort of knowledge to note about a lamp-post that it has a
lamp.

Now secular education really means that everybody shall
make a point of looking down at the pavement, lest by some
fatal chance somebody should look up at the lamp. The
lamp of faith that did in fact illuminate the street for the mass
of mankind in most ages of history, was not only a wandering
fire seen floating in the air by visionaries; it was also for most
people the explanation of the post. If a low cloud like a
London fog must indeed cover that flame, then it is an objective fact that the object will remain chiefly as an object to

be bumped into. I am not blaming anybody who can only manage to regard the world in that highly objective light. Even if the lamp-post appears as a post without a lamp, and therefore a post without a purpose, it may be possible to take different views of it. The stoic, like the tramp, may lean on it; the optimist, like the drunkard, may embrace it; the progressive may attempt to climb it, and so on. So it is with those who merely bump into a headless world as into a lampless post; to whom the world is a large objective obstacle. I only say that there is a difference, and not a small or secondary difference, between those who know and those who do not know what the post is for.

The deepest of all desires for knowledge is the desire to know what the world is for and what we are for. Those who believe they can answer that question must at least be allowed to answer it as the first question and not as the last. A man who cannot answer it has a right to refuse to answer it; though perhaps he is rather too prone to comfort himself with the very dogmatic dogma that nobody else can answer it if he can't. But no man has a right to answer it, or even to arrange for it being answered, as if it were a sort of peculiar and pedantic additional question, which only a peculiar and pedantic sort of pupil would be likely to ask. Secular education is more sensible than making religion one of the extras; like learning fret-work or Portuguese. And this principle is important in the controversy about religious education, because it involves the whole question which was so prominent in the controversy, the question of what is called 'atmosphere'. All that it means is, that anybody who has a right to answer this question has a right to answer it as if it were the sort of question that it is; a question affecting the nature of the whole world and the purpose of every part of human life. If a man is to teach religion, it is absurd to ask him to teach it as if it were something else, that did not apply to all the activities of man. The expression 'a religious hour' is something very like a contradiction in terms. And it is amusing to note that the same casual sceptic who is always sneering at the orthodox for their forms and limitations, who is always talking of their Sunday religion and their separation of things sacred and profane, is generally the very man who is most ready to make fun of the idea of a religious atmosphere in the schools. That is to say he of all people objects most to sacred and profane things being united and to a religion that works on week-days as well as on Sundays. The truth is that the idea of atmosphere is simply a piece of the elementary psychology of children. In any other matter, these people would be the first to tell us that education must take note of all the influences forming the mind, however apparently light or accidental. They will go wild with dismay if the child has to look at the wrong wall-paper; they will set themselves seriously to see that he has the right picture of the wombat; but they tell us not to trouble whether he has the right picture of the world.

I am not implying, of course, that there is no value in a secular social enthusiasm; or even that, in the language that some use sincerely and even usefully, it may not deserve to be called religion. What I doubt is whether it can in this sense deserve to be called reason. It does not satisfy the primary intellectual hunger about the meaning of life, that certain people may mean well, even when they doubt whether it means anything. The truth is that there is implied in almost all idealism a number of ideas which the idealists have seldom really followed out as ideas. There is the notion of a choice that is mysteriously offered and followed by equally mysterious consequences; of a mystical value attached to one part of our nature without any authority to value it; of a sort of ultimate tryst with nobody in particular; in short all the rich tints of a London fog surrounding a lamp-post without a lamp. I am very far from lacking in respect for all this groping idealism; I only say, that by its own confession, it is very incomplete compared with that of anybody who has a complete philosophy, because he has a creed. And I mean no offence when I say that anybody who has this sort of education is literally a half-educated person.

But there is another aspect of the case, which illustrates the real truth in the rather rustic Puritanism of the people who made a fuss about Darwinism in Dayton. To some of us it seems strange that such very antiquated Protestantism should be supposed to represent religion. It seems stranger that such very antiquated Darwinism should be supposed to represent science. But as a matter of fact the protest and prosecution on that occasion did represent something. It stood for a strong popular instinct, not without justification, that science is being made to mean more than science ever really says. An evolutionary education is something very different from an education about evolution. Just as a religious school openly and avowedly gives a religious atmosphere, as a scientific class does sometimes covertly or unconsciously give a materialistic atmosphere. A secularist teacher has just as much difficulty as a priest would have, in not giving his own answer to the questions that are most worth answering. He also is a little annoyed at not being allowed to put the first things first. He tends more and more to turn his science into a philosophy. It makes the matter too disputable and provocative perhaps to call that philosophy materialistic. It is more polite and equally pointed to call it monistic. But the point is that this philosophy has in it something altogether alien, not only to all religions that refer back to the will of God, but even to all moralities that revolve upon the will of man. Rightly or wrongly, its image of the universe is not that of a post put up with the design of having a lamp on it; it is rather that of a post that grew like a tree; a lamp-post that eventually grew its own lamp. Now considering this vision of vague growth simply as an atmosphere and an impression on the minds of the young, (apart from its truth or falsehood) there is no doubt that it tends so far as it goes to the notion of most things being much of a muchness, being all equally inevitable fruits of the same tree; and certainly not towards the idea of moral choice and conflict; of a contrast between black and white or a battle between light and darkness.

I am not writing controversially or trying to pin anybody with this as an individual necessity. I am writing educationally and considering the probable psychological impression of certain atmospheres and fine shades. I say that a great deal of evolution in education would not make that education very insistent on the ideas of free will and fighting morality; of dramatic choice and challenge. Why should one fruit challenge another fruit on the same tree; or how can there be a black and white choice between its slow gradations of green? So that even if we ignore the primary question of religion in the sense of the purpose of creation, there is the same sort of problem about religion even if we use it in the sense of the purpose of doing good. If a man believes that there is between vice and virtue a chasm like that of life and death, he will want to say so. And if other people only say that everything is a growth of evolution, he will not admit that they have said what he wishes to say. It is not merely a question of secular education that seems indifferent to religion, but of scientific education that seems rather indifferent to ethics. I am talking about educational effects, as educationists do; and decline any sort of sentimental recrimination about the pure and noble aims of men of science. Many who would despise anything so classical as the teaching of rhetoric, are always ready with any amount of rhetoric in praise of the teaching of science. I am not attacking the teaching of science, still less the teachers of science; I am saying the teaching of evolution, if it becomes an atmosphere, cannot be an atmosphere favourable to moral fire or a fighting spirit. To put it shortly, the teaching of evolution is hardly the training for revolution.

It is hardly likely to give a special strength to the feeling that some things are intrinsically intolerable or other things imperatively just. When a reformer can only say to a slave-driver, "You are evolving too slow; you ought to have emerged from the slave-state," the slave-driver has only to answer, "You are evolving too fast; you ought to wait for the twenty-first century." Such an argument will hardly set in a flame the fanaticism of Harper's Ferry. It seems to me, therefore, that the poor Puritans of Tennessee are not altogether wrong, as a matter of educational psychology, if they say that evolutionary education, even if it is not an attack on Christian doctrine, may become an atmosphere very alien to Christian morals; or indeed any manly and combative sort of morals. After the doctrine that existence is a thing of design, the next most interesting doctrine is that life is a thing of choice; and even if men were all taught to be atheists, I doubt whether mere evolutionism would have taught them to be really spirited and warlike atheists. And to see atheists lose their one great virtue of ferocity would indeed be a serious loss to religion.

THE PHILOSOPHY OF ISLANDS

Suppose that in some convulsion of the planets there fell upon this earth from Mars, a creature of a shape totally unfamiliar, a creature about whose actual structure we were of necessity so dark that we could not tell which was creature and which was clothes. We could see that it had, say, six red tufts on its head, but we should not know whether they were a highly respectable head-covering or simply a head. We should see that the tail ended in three yellow stars, but it would be difficult for us to know whether this was part of a ritual or simply a tail. Well, man has been from the beginning of time this unknown monster. People have always differed about what part of him belonged to himself, and what part was merely an accident. People have said successively that it was natural to him to do everything and anything that was diverse and mutually contradictory; that it was natural to him to worship God, and natural to him to be an atheist; natural to him to drink water, and natural to him to drink wine; natural to him to be equal, natural to be unequal; natural to obey kings, natural to kill them. The divergence is quite sufficient to justify us in asking if there are not many things that are really natural, which really appear early and strong in every normal human being, which are not embodied in any of his after affairs. Whether there are not morbidities which are as fresh and recurrent as the flowers of spring. Whether there are not superstitions whose darkness is as wholesome as the darkness that falls nightly on all living things. Whether we have not treated things essential as portents; whether we have not seen the sun as a meteor, a star of ill-luck.

It would at least appear that we tend to become separated from what is really natural, by the fact that we always talk about those people who are really natural as if they were goblins. There are three classes of people, for instance, who are in a greater or less degree elemental: children, poor people, and to some extent, and in a darker and more terrible manner, women. The reason why men have from the beginning of literature talked about women as if they were more or less mad, is simply because women are natural, and men, with their formalities and social theories, are very artificial. It is the same with children; children are simply human beings who are allowed to do what everyone else really desires to do, as for instance, to fly kites, or when seriously wronged to emit prolonged screams for several minutes. So again, the poor man is simply a person who expends upon treating himself and his friends in public houses about the same proportion of his income as richer people spend on dinners or cabs; that is, a great deal more than he ought. But nothing can be done until people give up talking about these people as if they were too eccentric for us to understand, when, as a matter of fact, if there is any eccentricity involved, we are too eccentric to understand them. A poor man, as it is weirdly ordained, is definable as a man who has not got much money; to hear philanthropists talk about him one would think he was a kangaroo. A child is a human being who has not grown up; to hear educationists talk one would think he was some variety of a deep-sea fish. The case of the sexes is at once more obvious and more difficult. The stoic philosophy and the early church discussed woman as if she were an institution, and in many cases decided to abolish her. The modern feminine output of literature discusses man as if he were an institution, and decides to abolish him. It can only timidly be suggested that neither man nor woman is an institution, but things that are really quite natural and all over the place.

If we take children, for instance, as examples of the un-corrupted human animal, we see that the very things which appear in them in a manner primary and prominent, are the very things that philosophers have taught us to regard as sophisticated and over-civilized. The things which really come first are the things which we are accustomed to think come last. The instinct for a pompous intricate and recurring ceremonial, for instance, comes to a child like an organic hunger; he asks for a formality as he might ask for a drink of water.

Those who think, for instance, that the thing called superstition is something heavily artificial, are very numer-ous; that is those who think that it has only been the power of priests or of some very deliberate system that has built up boundaries, that has called one course of action lawful and another unlawful, that has called one piece of ground sacred and another profane. Nothing it would seem, except a large and powerful conspiracy could account for men so strangely distinguishing between one field and another, between one city and another, between one nation and another. To all those who think in this way there is only one answer to be given. It is to approach each of them and whisper in his ear: "Did you or did you not as a child try to step on every alternate paving-stone? Was that artificial and a super-stition? Did priests come in the dead of night and mark out by secret signs the stones on which you are allowed to tread? Were children threatened with the oubliette or the fire of Smithfield if they failed to step on the right stone? Has the Church issued a bill "*Quisquam non pavemente?*" No! On this point on which we were really free, we invented our servi-tude. We chose to say that between the first and the third paving-stone there was an abyss of the eternal darkness into which we must not fall. We were walking along a steady and safe and modern road, and it was more pleasant to us to say that we were leaping desperately from peak to peak. Under mean and oppressive systems it was no doubt our instinct to free ourselves. But this truth written on the paving-stones is of even greater emphasis, that under liberal systems it was our instinct to limit ourselves. We limited ourselves so gladly that we limited ourselves at random, as if limitation were one of the adventures of boyhood.

People sometimes talk as if everything in the religious history of man had been done by officials. In all probability things like the Dionysian cult or the worship of the Virgin were almost entirely forced by the people on the priesthood. And if children had been sufficiently powerful in the State, there is no reason why this paving-stone religion should not have been accepted also. There is no reason why the streets up which we walk should not be emblazoned so as to commemorate the memory of a superstition as healthy as health itself.

For what is the idea in human nature which lies at the back of this almost automatic ceremonialism? Why is it that a child who would be furious if told by his nurse not to walk off the kerbstone, invents a whole desperate system of footholds and chasms in a plane in which his nurse can see little but a commodious level? It is because man has always had the instinct that to isolate a thing was to identify it. The flag only becomes a flag when it is unique; the nation only becomes a nation when it is surrounded; the hero only becomes a hero when he has before him and behind him men who are not heroes; the paving-stone only becomes a paving stone when it has before it and behind it things that are not paving stones.

There are two other obvious instances, of course, of the same instinct; the perennial poetry of islands, and the perennial poetry of ships. A ship like the Argo or the Fram is valued by the mind because it is an island, because, that is, it carries with it, floating loose on the desolate elements, the resources, and rules and trades, and treasuries of a nation, because it has ranks, and shops and streets, and the whole clinging like a few limpets to a lost spar. An island like Ithaca or England is valued by the mind because it is a ship, because it can find itself alone and self-dependent in a waste of water, because its orchards and forests can be numbered like bales of merchandise, because its corn can be counted like gold, because the starriest and dreariest snows upon its most forsaken peaks are silver flags flown from familiar masts, because its dimmest and most inhuman mines of coal or lead below the roots of things are definite chattels stored awkwardly in the lowest locker of the hold.

In truth, nothing has so much spoilt the right artistic attitude as the continual use of such words as 'infinite' and 'immeasurable'. They were used rightly enough in religion, because religion, by its very nature, consists of paradoxes. Religion speaks of an identity which is infinite, just as it spoke of an identity that was at once one and three, just as it might possibly and rightly speak of an identity that was at once black and white.

The old mystics spoke of an existence without end or a happiness without end, with a deliberate defiance, as they might have spoken of a bird without wings or a sea without water. And in this they were right philosophically, far more right than the world would now admit because all things grow more paradoxical as we approach the central truth. But for all human imaginative or artistic purposes nothing worse could be said of a work of beauty than that it is infinite; for to be infinite is to be shapeless, and to be shapeless is to be something more than mis-shapen. No man really wishes a thing which he believes to be divine to be in this earthly sense infinite. No one would really like a song to last for ever, or a religious service to last for ever, or even a glass of good ale to last for ever. And this is surely the reason that men have pursued towards the idea of holiness, the course that they have pursued; that they have marked it out in particular spaces, limited it to particular days, worshipped an ivory statue, worshipped a lump of stone. They have desired to give to it the chivalry and dignity of definition, they have desired to save it from the degradation of infinity. This is the real weakness of all imperial or conquering ideals in nationality. No one can love his country with the particular affection which is appropriate to the relation, if he thinks it is a thing in its nature indeterminate, something which is growing in the night, something which lacks the tense excitement of a boundary. No Roman citizen could feel the same when once it became possible for a rich Parthian or a rich Carthaginian to become a Roman citizen by waving his hand. No man wishes the thing he loves to grow, for he does not wish it to alter. No man would be pleased if he came home in the evening from work and found his wife eight feet high.

The dangers upon the side of this transcendental insularity are no doubt considerable. There lies in it primarily the great danger of the thing called idolatry, the worship of the object apart from or against the idea it represents. But he must surely have had a singular experience who thinks that this insular or idolatrous fault is the particular fault of one age. We are likely to suffer primary painful resemblance to the men of Thermopylae, the Zealots, who raged round the fall of Jerusalem. If we are rushing upon any destruction it is not, at least, upon this.

ON HOLIDAYS

THERE ARE epochs of history which their enemies call rude and which their friends call simple. My difficulty is that they seem to me not simple, but subtle. They understood much better than we do the idea of variety and reaction. For them emancipation was a recoil and not merely a release. The world must be turned upside down at absolute intervals, as a bucket must be turned upside down in order to empty it. It is the essence of a holiday that it must be a revolution, and it is the essence of a revolution that it must revolve. A revolution far more frightful and overwhelming than any of the revolutions of history happens every twelve hours. We do, quite seriously, die daily. We trust ourselves in utter dark and dissolution; in such black sleep as has killed many men by a drug or by the drifting snow. Each of us has every night an enormous negative holiday. But most will agree, I think, that the essence of that holiday is its irresponsibility. The legal authorities would be kept busy if we could be indicted for the crimes we have committed in dreams. Now the whole point of a holiday was to be, within certain rational restraints, irresponsible. Interfering with a holiday was almost like interfering with a dream. And the whole project of using holidays as anything else but holidays was really absent from the mind. The notion of 'combining amusement with instruction' would have seemed like the notion of combining sleep with insomnia. Great spiritual authorities have told us to watch and pray. Great spiritual influences, I think, also tell us to believe and sleep. But neither god nor priest nor devil ever had the impudence to tell us to watch and sleep.

And that is the contradiction made by the modern cranks about holidays. It would be a typical and triumphant work of modern science to take charge of a child day and night; to give him the drugs that would keep him half asleep all day, and the dreams that would keep him half awake all night.

In this connection I think the educational arrangement about holidays has long been a ludicrous mistake. Holiday tasks are a mistake. Home-work is a mistake. Give the boy or girl less holidays if you think they need less. But be sufficiently businesslike to get the best out of the boy or girl for whatever concession you make to them. If you can excuse anyone from work, you can excuse him from worry. Leisure is a food, like sleep; liberty is a food, like sleep. Leisure is a matter of quality rather than quantity. Five minutes lasts longer when one cannot be disturbed than five hours when one may be disturbed. Restrict the liberty in point of time; restrict it in point of space; but do not restrict it in point of quality. If you give somebody only three seconds' holiday – then, by all the remains of your ruined sense of honour, leave him alone for three seconds.

Let me take an example which involves a particular sort of holiday that is fairly popular and national. During the summer, the big railway stations will be found thronged with the bags and babies of innumerable families going to seaside resorts. Each traveller is (I need hardly say) murmuring to himself the lines of Swinburne:

"I will go down to the great white mother . . .
Mother and maker of men, the sea;
I will go down to her, I and none other . . ."

A friend of mine regards these lines as unreasonable, declaring that Swinburne, however much he liked sea-bathing, should not insist on all the seas of the world being locked up like his private bathroom. But certainly the request, whether reasonable or not, would be very difficult to enforce, say, at

Margate or Broadstairs. But even if it be true, as I were loth to believe, that some holiday-makers do not murmur Swinburne's lines as they start, I am still firmly convinced that most holiday-makers like the sea because it is some kind of outlook upon some kind of loneliness and liberty. It is the only kind of loneliness and liberty. It is the only plain, straight line in Nature. It is the only empty place on earth. It is the one open window; to Jones, as it was to Keats.

I think it was Richard Jefferies who said that all men ought to be idle; and that we should get all the work we wanted done by harnessing to our machinery the tremendous tides of the sea. Something analogous was suggested by Mr. Wells; but I disagree with it. I think it would destroy the holiday. We should have removed all the use of the seaside by removing the uselessness of the sea. Men jaded or dazed with duties wish to look out across that fruitless field, in which God has sown we know not what seed and shall raise we know not what harvest. They wish to behold how enormous is their irresponsibility. The sea blows upon the cashier at Margate the great good news that he is not God. But this holiday sentiment will continue to weaken so long as men try to make all our holidays duties, or all our days holidays; and cannot understand that when anything is being woven the shuttle flies back and forth.

THE PEASANT

THE GENIUS who shall write a real philosophical pantomime (a thing untried, I think, since Aristophanes) should
find many handy symbols in the harlequinades of our youth.
The donkey who comes in two suggests infinite speculations
about organic unity and by divergent evolution. The policeman made into sausages would be excellent machinery
either for a Socialistic satire or for a satire on Socialism. And
the red-hot poker quite exactly expresses that most terrible
and profound thing in human affairs – a fierce domesticity.

But there is another trick of the old pantomimes which
happens to offer the only parallel I can think of to the
strange state of our society today. We all remember that
beginning of the Transformation Scene when the front
scene is still there, but the back scene begins to glow through
it. The heroine is still in the dungeon; but the walls grow
more and more transparent; and something else (probably
the Garden of the Fairy Volatile) is apparent at the same
time.

I have exactly the same sensations about our old Victorian
political methods and the social realities that are now behind
them. I do not ignore the old front scene of Privy Council or
Parliament; I can still see it there; it is the England of my
boyhood, and I rather like it. But simultaneously with these
symbolic figures, these representatives and estates of the
realm, I can see the Things that are behind. Another England is shining through political England; whether it will be
very like the Garden of the Fairy Volatile remains to be seen.

This fact, that the Government and the Commonwealth

are often on two different planes of reality, has one peculiar result, too little noticed, on our attitude towards foreigners. There are the same names all over Europe – Parliament, Army, Church, Land, and so on. But these words often stand for astonishingly different things; for widely varying degrees of realism or ritual or memory or conspiracy or indifference. When a man has even one concrete experience of some foreign thing, he will generally find it to be in quite another world from that foreign country as it appears in the newspapers. A man reading the best English journals would have the general impression that the chief event in France is the sudden fall of the Ministry which came as abruptly as that tragic blow out of the air which a few weeks before had struck one of its members dead where he stood.

Now I happened to be in France when the news of this tragedy was scattered abroad, and I want to try and convey an atmosphere which I felt, and which I felt to be France itself. To us in England France seemed to be full of all this crisis and disaster. This was something like what one felt upon the actual scene of it.

I was away in those eastern highlands, where France (so to speak) clings to the rising mountains, till they break away and shoot up into the sky as Switzerland. More to the north was that gap that is the great gate into Germany and is guarded by the Lion of Belfort. Among these hills I met a peasant who was like thousands of the peasants all round: a Jack-of-all-trades. Among other things he owned a ramshackle carriage with an excellent horse, with which he could drive me anywhere; and he was, as far as appearance goes, rather like a very rude beggar. His clothes were coarse and threadbare, his face was rugged, but sharp; he was always in a sweat from drudgeries. A man who looked like that would be 'moved on' in London if he tried to open the door of a cab. Well, I got him to drive me away over the hills, and, finding that the mountains grew taller, grander, and (one might say) more incredible at every turn of the road, I persuaded him to make a day's journey of it, and to rest the horse in a high village where (as everywhere in that country) one could get good wine and bread and an omelette at least.

Now, when I stopped before the cottage that could thus become an impromptu inn, I did exactly what every Englishman of my unfortunate class would have done in my place. I addressed the driver with nervous cordiality and extreme vagueness and said that I supposed he would like to have some lunch too, offering him a few francs for the purpose. He did not understand what it meant. He said I had better pay for the carriage at the end. I said it again, and still it was a puzzle to him. I said it again, in French which, however bad, was at least unmistakable; and this time I made myself clear. Whereupon this amazing scarecrow burst into an ungovernable fit of laughter, and slapped his trouser pocket about six times with his squat spread hand, exclaiming, "Money! I have much! I have mountains! I am rich! I am very rich!" And after the conversation I had with him on the road home, I think it perfectly possible that he was considerably richer than I am.

He talked about his dog, which was the best dog in the world; his son, who was the most promising cook in the world; his horse, which was the most astonishing horse in the world; he seemed to find inexhaustible glories in his patch of property. At the end of the journey, warned by that prodigy of the noon, I offered him no extra tip, but only two good cigars that somebody had given me. He at once replied by giving me a bottle of the wine he manufactured himself. It was, he assured me, the best wine in the world.

That is all that happened; only as we drove into the town the papers were flaring with the dreadful death of the French Minister of War and the narrow escape of the French Premier. My friend had never heard of either of them; he took no interest in politics. I think he thought politics a sort of mutiny among slaves. He was a free man. I think my sociological friends really ought to remember that there are many millions of him in Europe.

THE LOST RAILWAY STATION

I AM writing this as best I may in a Scottish railway station; and my thoughts go back, with all the pathos of the patriot, to an English railway station. Trucks and rails may seem to lack the fine shades of variety to be felt in the trees and hills of home; but my fancy really flies to an English railway station where I once dreamed a dream.

There is in the north of London an important station, which is by comparison as quiet and comfortable as the courtyard of an old inn. I do not know why this repose rests upon it, for a considerable train service is connected with it. It has the usual bookstall, at which I have bought all the bloodiest detective stories I could find; various refreshment bars at which I have bought various other things; and all the usual fittings of such a place. But in the centre there stands a fountain, and not far from it a large model of an ocean liner. Something about the look of the fountain and the surrounding hostelries, jutting out on opposite sides, reminds me absurdly of the market-place of a village; though perhaps something of a pantomime village. I can imagine the village maiden leaning gracefully on the fountain with a jar or jug or bucket; though I hasten to admit that I have never seen her do so. I can even conceive that the little boy who ran away to sea (that picturesque figure, whose presence, or rather absence, is so essential to the health of the happy village) drank in all his desire of seafaring adventure at the ends of the earth by looking at the toy liner. His white-haired mother would still be waiting for him – presumably in the waiting-room. In short, I have always felt that I could fill this place with all the recognized romantic figures of rural life, in fiction if not in fact.

I wonder what would really happen if in some special convulsion that station were really cut off and left to live its own simple life, like a farm surrounded by floods, or a hamlet snowed up in the mountains. It pleases me to fancy that a railway strike might go on so long that people forgot the very purpose of a railway station. Railway porters would not even know that they were railway porters; and even the station-master would be ignorant of the mysterious secret of his mastery. Most of us have had a fancy that all society is like that strange railway station; that its social actions have some hieratic significance lost before the beginning of history; that it was made it knows not why; and is waiting for it knows not what. For the end of such a play or parable would be something truly terrific, like the Day of Judgment. When the signals changed colours at last, it would truly be like the moon turning to blood in the Apocalypse. Something utterly unthinkable, like the thunder and the seals and trumpets of the Last Day, would transform my quiet railway-station. A train would come in at last.

But my fancy chiefly rests on the remote generations of the future in this simple community, descended from the original primitive marriages between a few railway porters and a few barmaids. By that time the little commonwealth ought to have a whole tangle of traditions ultimately to be traced back to the lost idea of a train. Perhaps people would still go religiously to the ticket-office at intervals, as to a kind of confessional box; and there recite the names of far-off and by this time fabulous places; the word 'Harrow' sounding like the word 'Heaven' or the word 'Ealing' like the word 'Eden'. For this society would of course, like every other, produce sceptics; that is men who had lost their social memory. All sorts of quaint ceremonials would survive, and would be scoffed at as irrational, because their rational origin had been obscured. At a date centuries hence, the clock in the refreshment room would still be kept a little fast, as compared with the clock in the station. There would be most complicated controversies about this custom; turning on things behind the times and things in advance of the age. The bookstall would have come to be something like the Bodleian or the great lost library of Alexandria; a storehouse of ancestral documents of primitive antiquity and profound obscurity; and learned men would be found spelling their way through a paragraph in one of our daily papers, deluded with the ever-vanishing hope of finding a sort of human meaning in it. The fountain seems to be the only possible religious centre of the village; though I think the mysterious image of the great ship should be the type of some faint adventurous memory and adventurous hope; a vague hint of things beyond; perhaps a great legend like that of the Argo. But a fountain is clearly the more human and historic site for a shrine. It would be dedicated, I hope, to a saint; as are so many springs and wells all over Christendom. And now I come to think of it, the very name of this railway station, like so much also that sounds cockney and commonplace, has an origin presumably religious. There could hardly be a more beautiful combination of words and ideas than that which I imagine to lie behind the prosaic name of Marylebone.

I had intended to draw a moral, or many morals from this vision. I had intended to point out how much our own society suffers from a similar paradox; not that its institutions are meaningless; but on the contrary, that they have a meaning, which would be found again if the society woke up and went to work again. It is only because they are asleep that they seem to be senseless. If the trains were running, if the traditions were working, the traditions would be instantly recognized as reasonable. Thus the modern world does not really suffer from scurry, but rather from slumber. I had in mind especially what I may call the Allegory of the

Lost Luggage, or of the Cloak Room, which is concerned with the philosophy of property. Property is still being defended by a dim sense of duty; though it is really held up in transit and accumulated in the wrong place. But I cannot pursue my guess; for something has happened in the Scotch railway station which dissipates all my dreams of the happier English railway station. My train has come in.

BETHLEHEM AND THE GREAT
CITIES

I was once at the same dinner-table with a newspaper proprietor who regarded himself, and was regarded, as the dictator of Europe and who really was by far too great an extent the dictator of England. He also was interested in Palestine, and in the course of conversation I learned that he had never even heard of the Latin kingdom of Jerusalem. I suppose he had seen Crusaders in pictures or at fancy-dress balls; but he had no notion of what they did, and certainly no notion that what they did was to conquer and make Palestine a part of Europe for a hundred years, filling it with abbeys like those of Glastonbury or St. Andrew's and castles like those of Conway and Caernarvon. Now that is a point that interests me a great deal because the traces of it are very obvious to any traveller who happens to have been there. The first fact that strikes him about Jerusalem is that it is a medieval town; long before it strikes him specially as an oriental town. It has that curious combination of cosiness and defiance that belongs to the walled cities and painted pales and fences of the life of the Middle Ages. The latest walls were built by the successors of the Saracens but they are not in our sense Saracenic. Most of the windows and gates are in their whole spirit Gothic. The Franciscan going by with his beard and brown habit under those grey Gothic walls seems to be entirely in the picture, and even in the conventional picture. It is rather the Arab coming in with his coloured turban or burnous who seems for the moment, if only by a sort of optical illusion, to be a stranger and one straying from a far-off eastern land.

I had a rather parallel experience when I first saw Rome. In the case of Rome, as in the case of Jerusalem, people seem to have lost their own first impressions in the disproportionate emphasis of detail among guides and guide-books. The general impression of Rome is not the Forum or even the Coliseum. We might almost say that they are to St. Peter's what Stonehenge is to Salisbury Cathedral. The overwhelming impression is not that of Pagan but of Papal Rome; but especially Rome of the Renaissance Popes. I say it is the overwhelming impression; it could not be to everybody a pleasing impression. It might annoy a man, not only if he were narrowly Puritan, but also if he were too narrowly medieval. It did annoy Ruskin and might well have annoyed William Morris. Nor is their criticism a thing merely to be criticized; there is in that classical exuberance much that is really florid and false. But that *is* the impression; and it is quite certainly the stamp and imprint of the great Popes of the Renaissance. Renaissance Rome is not merely heathen, any more than Jerusalem is merely Jewish or merely Moslem. In those huge fountains where the Tritons look like Titans in the twilight, they have none the less been really baptized by these waters. The cross on top of the primeval obelisks is not a contradiction but a culmination. The culmination culminates on that high column where Our Lady stands at once vanquishing and exalting the symbol of Diana, with her foot upon the horns of the moon.

I have mentioned these two cases for the sake of a truth which any real traveller will have found out for himself. Our recent and rather provincial tradition greatly exaggerated the proportion of such places that is pagan or barbaric or even merely primeval. There is much more than we were taught to suppose of the traces of civilization, and even of our own civilization. But as my memory returns to Palestine by this rambling path, I remember what may really be called, in a deeper and more subtle sense, an exception. Palestine itself was filled, so to speak, with Norman castles and Catholic shrines; and in so far as Jerusalem does often suggest the Moslem, it is chiefly because the Moslem does suggest the Crusaders. But there was one experience in Palestinian travel that really is something more than merely historical; something that is too human to be historical. It is certainly not pagan but it is in a sense primeval. It is the one thing that really does seem to be connected with Christianity and not with Christendom. I have called it primeval, because there is in this greatest of all origins an atmosphere truly to be called original. This one vision really does not primarily suggest pilgrimages and shrines and medieval spires or medieval spears. It does rather suggest ancestral dawns and mystical abysses and the end of chaos and the creation of light. I mean the experience of Bethlehem.

The heart of Bethlehem is a cavern; the sunken shrine which is the traditional scene of the Nativity. Nine times out of ten these traditions are true, and this is wholly ratified by the truth about the countryside; for it is into such subterranean stables that the people have driven their cattle, and they are by far the likeliest places of refuge for such a homeless group. It is curious to consider what numberless and varied versions of the Bethlehem story have been turned into pictures. No man who understands Christianity will complain that they are all different from each other and all different from the truth, or rather the fact. It is the whole point of the story that it happened in one particular human place that might have been any particular human place; a sunny colonnade in Italy or a snow-laden cottage in Sussex. It is yet more curious that some modern artists have prided themselves on merely topographical truth; and yet have not made much of this truth about the dark and sacred place underground. It seems strange that they have hardly emphasized the one case in which realism really touches reality. There is something beyond expression moving to the imagination in the idea of the holy fugitives being brought lower than the very land; as if the earth had swallowed them; the glory of God like gold buried in the ground. Perhaps the image is too deep for art, even in the sense of dealing in another dimension. For it might be difficult for any art to convey simultaneously the divine secret of the cavern and the cavalcade of the mysterious kings, trampling the rocky plain and shaking the cavern roof. Yet the medieval pictures would often represent parallel scenes on the same canvas; and the medieval popular theatre, which the guildsmen wheeled about the streets, was sometimes a structure of three floors, with one scene above another. A parallel can be found in those tremendous lines of Francis Thompson:

> East, ah, east of Himalay
> Dwell the nations underground,
> Hiding from the shock of Day;
> From the sun's uprising sound.

But no poetry even of the greatest poets will ever express all that is hidden in that image of the light of the world like a subterranean sun; only these prosaic notes remain to suggest what one individual felt about Bethlehem.

THE SACREDNESS OF SITES

IT IS impossible to make a list of the things that humanitarians do not know about humanity. On thousands of things the men who talk most of the common bond are ignorant of what is really common. Among a thousand of such things may be mentioned the instinct about the sacredness of sites. If there is one thing that men have proved again and again it is that even when they furiously burn down a temple, they like to put another on top of it. They do not, generally speaking, want to worship St. George except on the very spot where they once worshipped the Dragon. And even when they have altered the universe they do not alter the situation. What is the reason for this, and whether it is some hitherto nameless need of human nature, or whether there be indeed something behind those ancient legends of the *genius loci*, or spirit of the place, need not now be discussed. But it is certain that throughout all history there has been a rhythm of expansion and contraction from certain centres; and that, unless we would be as superficial as the shallowest journalists, we can see under all changes that these centres remain. It is commonplace that empires pass away, because empires were never very important. Empires are frivolous things, the fringes of a sprawling culture that has sprawled too far. Cities do not pass away, or very seldom pass away, because the city is the cell of our organic formation; and even those living in the vast void of empire can find no phrase for social duty, save to tell men to be good citizens.

Empires pass away almost as if to accentuate the fact that cities do not pass away. At least five empires have successively claimed suzerainty over little Jerusalem upon the hill; and they are all now mere names – Egypt and Babylon and Persia and Macedonia and Rome; and for those unaffected by names these are unimportant. But Jerusalem is not unimportant; it is, at this very moment when I write, the scene of surging and threatening conflict. There was a Byzantine Empire and there is still a Turkish Empire, and one may soon be as dead as the other; but it will always matter who holds San Sophia and the town of Constantine upon the Golden Horn. Paris is older than France and York is older than England; and Cologne is immeasurably older than Germany. These centres of civilization have something in them more magnetic and immortal even than nationality, let alone mere vulgar imperialism. Ghosts haunt houses, they say, and the ghosts of whole people haunt whole cities, till half Europe is like a haunted house. It is only dull materialists who can wander away into any material environment. The spirit and all that is spiritual returns to its own environment. The world ebbs back again to its cities, to its centres; it is true, as I have said, of many cities; it is most true of the most central city of Rome.

Everything was done to take away the Roman character from Rome. The Emperor was taken away, but the Pope remained. The Pope was taken away, but the Pope returned. The former could not make a new Rome at Byzantium. The latter could not make a new Rome at Avignon. The former experiment had behind it the great civilization of the Greeks, the latter had behind it the great civilization of the French. The Greek Emperors thought they could move it easily to the East and the French Kings that they could move it easily to the West. But Rome, especially Christian Rome, is a rock not easily to be moved; and in the course of but a few centuries, as history goes, she had seen the French Monarchy go down before the Jacobins as she had seen the Greek Empire go down before the Moslems.

I am now about to utter a sentence of familiar and horrid cant, which I fear may be respectfully received. It is said everywhere, in a sense that is quite false; and yet, strangely enough, it is quite true. I am going to say that the world is not yet ready for enforced international peace and disarmament in Europe. In all the welter of wordy hypocrisy that makes so much of modern culture and moral science, I know nothing so contemptible, as a rule, as that evolutionary excuse about the world not being ripe. It is said by Socialists who do not want to leave off being Capitalists. It is said by war-profiteers who would like one more war to make them millionaires, and then eternal peace; or by high-minded gluttons and epicures who would like their grandchildren to be vegetarians. So the employer may go on sweating because the world is not ready for Communism; or the huckster may go on swindling because the social evolution of man has not yet reached the point of common honesty; or the politician may bribe and be bribed at leisure, because the social prophets have calculated an exact and distant date for Utopia. But they can all sweat and swindle, and bribe hopefully, happily, with radiant faces, because Utopia is sure to come some time – and for somebody else. Ninety times out of a hundred this moral distinction is false and cowardly; but in this special case, for one special reason, it does really apply. I doubt very much whether there will ever be a time when there will be no war. I cannot imagine how there can be a time in which there *can* be no war. But I do believe that, if the life of Europe evolves in one particular way, there may yet be something very like real European unity; an international understanding that would really prevent many international misunderstandings. But of that development it really is true to say that it has not happened yet, and that, until it has happened, we must not act as if it had.

Human unity is a huge and overwhelming truth, in the face of which all differences of continent or country are flattened out. European unity is an ancient fundamental and sometimes invisible truth, which every white man will discover if he meets another white man in Central Africa or unpenetrated Tibet. But national unity is a truth; and a truth which cannot, must not, and will not be denied, but chiefly for these very reasons – that nationality is human and that nationality is European. The man who forgets nationality instantly becomes less human and less European. He seems somehow to have turned into a walking abstraction, a resolution of some committee, a programme of some political movement, and to be by some unmistakable transformation, striking chill like the touch of a fish, less of a living man. The European man is a man through his patriotism and the particular civilization of his people. The cosmopolitan is not a European, still less a good European. He is a traveller in Europe, as if he were a tourist from the moon. In other words, what has happened is this; that for good or evil, European history has produced European nations by a European process; they are the organs of the organic life of our race, at least in recent times; and unless we receive our natural European inheritance through those natural organs, we do not really receive it at all. We receive something else; a priggish and provincial abstraction, invented by a few modern and more or less ignorant men. So long as those organs are the only organs of a living tradition, we must live by them; and it is true to say that the time has not yet come for all the nations living by a tradition that they can all hold and inherit together. It means finding something that good men love even more than they love their country. And modern Europe has not got it yet.

I will not argue here about how Europe is to get it; but I would suggest that it might possibly begin by returning to the civic origins. I mean that the countries may not expand to the continents, but rather return to the cities. Humanity may find in the cities what might yet become a universal citizenship, as it did with the cities of antiquity. But it could only happen with the cities that are really antique. It would mean the sort of cities which we only call ancient because they are still alive. But it would repose on the real and profoundly human sentiment about sites, for sites are generally shrines.

SCIPIO AND THE CHILDREN

I HAVE lately found myself in the town of Tarragona; famous for its vinegar, which it wisely sends abroad, rather than the wine, which it still more wisely drinks at home. I have myself ordered a fair amount of the wine; I omitted to order any of the vinegar. These things are an allegory; for there is something of the same contrast between the acid taste of party politics, especially anti-clerical politics, which is all that is exported to the English papers from Spain, and the rich and joyful vintage of popular life and humour, of which nobody can get the gusto except by going to Spain. I have always noted that there is never anything new in the news; and the things which the traveller recognizes are never the things that the journalist reports. For instance, the thing that struck me first and last in Spain was the Spanish children; especially the Spanish little boys, and their relation to the Spanish fathers of the Spanish little boys. The love of fathers and sons in this country is one of the great poems of Christendom; it has, like a bewildering jewel, a hundred beautiful aspects, and especially that supremely beautiful aspect; that it is a knock in the eye for that nasty-minded old pedant Freud.

I was sitting at a café table with another English traveller, and I was looking at a little boy with a bow and arrows, who discharged very random shafts in all directions, and periodically turned in triumph and flung himself into the arms of his father, who was a waiter. That part of the scene was repeated all over the place, with fathers of every social type and trade. And it is no good to tell me that such humanities must be peculiar to the progressive and enlightened Catalans, in that this incident happened in a Catalan town, for I happen to remember that I first noticed the fact in Toledo and afterwards even more obviously in Madrid. And it is no good to tell me that Spaniards are all gloomy and harsh and cruel, for I have seen the children; I have also seen the parents. I might be inclined to call them spoilt children; except that it seems as if they could not be spoilt. I may also remark that one element whch specially haunts me, in the Spanish Peninsula, is the very elusive element called Liberty. Nobody seems to have the itch of interference; nobody is moved by that great motto of so much social legislation; "Go and see what Tommy is doing, and tell him he mustn't." Considering what this Tommy was doing, I am fairly sure that in most progressive countries, somebody would tell him he mustn't. He shot an arrow that hit his father; probably because he was aiming at something else. He shot an arrow that hit me; but I am a BROAD target. His bow and his archery were quite inadequate; and would not have been tolerated in the scientific Archery School into which he would no doubt have been instantly drafted in any state in which sport is taken as seriously as it should be. While I was staring at him, and at some other little boys who had assembled, also to stare at him, the English traveller interrupted my dream by saying suddenly:

"What is there to *see* in Tarragona?"

I was instantly prompted to answer, and almost did answer, "Why, of course, the boy with the bow and arrows! There is also the waiter."

But I stopped myself in time, remembering the strange philosophy of sightseeing; and then I found my mind rather a blank. I knew next to nothing about the town, and said so. I said the Cathedral was very fine; and then added with increasing vagueness; "I'm afraid I don't know anything at all about Tarragona. I have a hazy idea that Scipio got buried here or born here. I can't even remember which."

"Who was it who was buried or born?" he inquired patiently.

"Scipio," I said, with an increasing sense of weakness; then I added as in feeble self-defence, "Africanus."

He inquired whether I meant that the man was an African. I feared, in any case, that the word 'African' would not instantly summon up before his imagination the figure of St. Augustine; or even of Hannibal. It would more probably suggest to him a coal-black negro. So I said that I was sure he was not an African; I believed he was a Roman; certainly he was a Roman General; and I thought it was too early in history for a Roman General to have really belonged to what were afterwards the Roman Provinces. I had always understood that Carthage, or the Carthaginian influence, practically prevailed over all these parts at that time. And even as I said the words a thought came to me, like a blinding and even a blasting light.

The traveller was very legitimately bored. After the mysterious manner of his kind, he was not bored with sightseeing, but he was bored with history; especially ancient history. I do not blame him for that; I only puzzle upon why a man bored with history should take endless trouble to visit historic sites. He was patently one of those who think that all those things happened such a long time ago that they cannot make much difference now. But it had suddenly occurred to me that this rather remote example really might, perhaps, make a great deal of difference now. I tried to tell him so; and he must have formed the impression that I was raving mad.

"Would it be all the same," I asked, "if that little boy were thrown into a furnace as a religious ceremony, when his family went to church on Sunday? That is what Carthage did; it worshipped Moloch; and sacrificed batches of babies

147

as a regular religious ritual. That is what Scipo Africanus did; he defeated Carthage, when it had nearly defeated the world. Somehow, I seem to feel a fine shade of difference."

My companion did not reply; and I continued to watch the archer; and though Apollo was a Pagan god, I am glad that such a sun-god slew the Punic Python; and that even before the Faith, those ancient arrows cast down Moloch for us all.

THE REAL ISSUE

THE FOLLOWING incident took place the other day outside a crowded café in Paris. It also took place outside half a hundred other cafés in Paris and half a million other cafés scattered through about two-thirds of Christendom. The incident or something like it, was so natural as to seem trivial in such places; and probably nobody noticed it except two persons seated near that one small table. One of them was a wealthy American lady who had seen the sights of Paris. The other was a journalist, astray in foreign parts, who had resolutely refused to see them.

There sat at this small table a poor Frenchman with his wife and child; he was rather shabbier than what we should call an artisan, but he was probably a small shopkeeper; he was independent; it had never occurred to him to pretend to be a gentleman. He and his wife each proceeded to sip a very tall glass of very light beer, called a bock, and to look out cheerfully at the coloured lights and the motley procession of mankind passing under them. The little boy threw his arms round his father's neck with sudden affection; for he was quite ignorant, had never read even the most elementary text-book of Psycho-Analysis and did not know anything about Oedipus. Then his father gave him, equally impulsively, a gulp out of his glass of beer. The little boy then turned and embraced his mother, who also, moved by a sense of symmetry and equality, gave him another gulp out of her glass of beer. At that moment a lame man came by begging; and the man at the table (who would have been turned away from many of our respectable houses as a beggar himself), took some small coins from his pocket and gave them to the child, with a few words in an undertone. The child then gave them to the beggar. That was all. But one of the two strangers in that city knew he had been looking at the palladium and high citadel, round which rages the whole human war of our civilization and our century; and that all men are divided precisely and sharply by what they think of that one thing. Those who understand it are on one side and those who do not understand it on the other. The former see a thousand things and generally say very little about them. They understand that ritual is natural and not artificial. They understand what is really meant by the equality of the sexes: "In this we both have a part and he in us, equally."

They understand that the world ends when that trinity is really broken, whether by confounding the persons or dividing the substance. They understand the word 'sacrament', which is simply senseless gibberish to everybody else. They understand that politics and economics and everything practical means providing the huge human café with such tables – but separate tables. They understand that when this has been done as fully and fairly as possible, there will still always be somebody limping by; and that he must not be forgotten. Above all, they understand the impulse that makes the most innocent the intermediary and the almoner; they understand propitiation and the priest.

There are also other kinds of people. For the well-dressed American rose from her table with a sort of snort and went on her way to see the sights of Paris. We must not be hard on her; in truth the poor lady suffered from delusions; for she laboured under the extraordinary notion that she had seen ignorant people giving a child Alcohol; and she was ridden with a sort of nightmare, to the effect that a beggar is a horrible thing.

THE COMIC CONSTABLE

Some little time ago a small, strange incident occurred to me which is not without its application to the history and quality of this country. I was sitting quietly in rustic retirement, endeavouring to feel as bucolic as possible, when I was summoned to the telephone, not perhaps the most bucolic of institutions. Nor, indeed, was it the voice of any other alehouse gaffer that addressed me through the instrument, but the voice of a man I know on one of the big London dailies. He said, "We hear you've been made Constable of Beaconsfield." I said, "Then your hearing is defective." He said after a pause. "Well, but *haven't* you been made Constable of Beaconsfield?" "Why, of course not," I said. "Have you been made Pope of Rome? Am I a person whom any sane men (except perhaps the criminals) would want to have for a constable?" "Well," replied my friend doubtfully, "It's down in the 'Daily Gazette', anyhow. 'Mr. G. K. Chesterton has been nominated as a Parish Constable of Beaconsfield.'" "And a jolly good joke, too," I answered. "I thought you had a more vivid and vulgar sense of humour." "We may take it, then, that the thing is a hoax?" said the inquisitor. "You may indeed," I said, "and apparently a successful one." I then hung up the receiver and went back and tried to feel bucolic again.

When I had tried for three minutes the telephone rang again. A well-known weekly illustrated paper had important business with me. "We hear," said a grave voice, "that you are now Parish Constable of Beaconsfield, and any experiences of yours in that capacity —" "I am not Parish

Constable of Beaconsfield," I cried in a tearful rage, "nor am I Senior Wrangler, nor Gold Stick in Waiting, nor the Grand Lama, nor the Living Skeleton, nor the Derby Favourite, nor the Queen of Love and Beauty at an approaching tournament. Has the human race lost all notion of a joke?"

I went back somewhat impatiently to my bucolic efforts; and then another bell rang, this time the front-door bell. I was informed that the representative of yet a third paper (an illustrated daily this time) had come down all the way from London with a camera to photograph me as a Parish Constable. I do not know whether he thought to find me in some flamboyant uniform, with feathers and epaulettes, or whether he merely wished to snapshot the new and rapturous expression of my face after receiving the appointment. Anyhow, I told him he was welcome to photograph me as much as he chose in the character of "The Man Who is not Parish Constable of Beaconsfield." He photographed me in a number of highly unconstabulary attitudes (calculated in themselves to refute the slander), and then he went away.

It happened that about a quarter of an hour afterwards a local Beaconsfield acquaintance dropped in for ten minutes' talk, and to him I recounted with mingled entertainment and fury how all these experienced journalists had been taken in by a joke that seemed to me as obvious as anything in a comic paper. "I suppose," I said, "that whenever *Punch* playfully suggests I caused the earthquake at San Francisco by sitting down in Beaconsfield, I shall have to write to *The Times* about it, and clear my character." My local friend listened with interest to the farce, laughed at the inquiring newspaper, was amiably amused at the disappointed photographer, and at the end said very quietly and casually. "All the same, you know, you *are* nominated as a Parish Constable of Beaconsfield."

I turned, stiff with astonishment; I saw the shocking

sincerity in his eyes, "But this is madness," I cried, "It *must* be a joke." "If it is," he said, apologetically, "it is a joke written up on the church door." My wits were scattered to the four winds; I collected them with difficulty. I could not fancy that those who go to a modern parish church would permit such a thing as a practical joke in the porch. It was no time for half measures, but rather for desperate ones. It was clearly necessary to go to church.

My friend and I walked to the stone entrance of that strong and fine building, and there, sure enough, stood in cold print the openly crazy statement that some five men, including Mr. G. K. Chesterton, had been nominated as Parish Constables, and that objections to them would be entertained. Unless Englishmen have lost their historic fire, those objections should be prompt and overwhelming. On the way back my friend fortified and consoled me by describing the institution which had thus forcibly descended on me like an extinguisher. I have since received a letter from a kind correspondent including much the same technicalities, for which I am very grateful; but at the time the explanation was a little confusing. The only thing I clearly remember out of the tangle of rules is this; that I must not go officially beyond the bounds of my Constablewick, "except in hot pursuit of a fugitive." I may be enticed to toss myself over a spiked wall into Middlesex; but only if a fleet-footed burglar has tossed himself over it before my eyes. I may be observed any day leaping across the Thames into Berkshire, but only when some panting bigamist has leapt it just before me. I can most earnestly and even austerely promise that on ordinary occasions I shall permit myself no such impetuous trespass.

But we will not dwell upon the duties, because there are no duties; nor upon the salary, because there is no salary; nor upon the uniform (the only thing I really regret) because, alas! there is no uniform. But if we consider the thing itself, and why so wild a joke ever came to be possible as the present writer being a constable, we may find ourselves facing some rather curious and interesting elements in the old life of England. The institution of the Parish Constable dates from the time when there was no official and efficient police; but when there was a great deal of incidental local sentiment and local self-government. In short, the Parish Constable belongs to another age, when there was not really such a thing as a constable, but when there was such a thing as a parish. The very form of his appointment breathes of a somewhat breezier age; for (as in my own case) he is not even asked if he will stand. This suggests the jolly time when there was no nonsense about wanting to serve your country; no buying of peerages by breeding cattle; no climbing into rich idleness by means of 'polite work'.

Doubtless it is august and dignified to be a constable. So it is august and dignified to be a juryman; for to be a juryman is to be a judge, but in nothing is the jury system more medieval (that is, more human) than in the fact that it takes for granted that every good man will primarily care more for his babies or his bullocks than for the codes and thrones of legality; and that, therefore, he must be *summoned* to a jury. That is perhaps what Christ meant when he described the Kingdom of Heaven as sending into the highways and byeways, and compelling them to come in; perhaps He meant that if you want the simple and modest mortal you must call him. However this may be with the Kingdom of Heaven, it is assuredly so with the Kingdom of Earth. The other method leaves us open to that offensive class which comes without being called, the vulgarly and basely ambitious, who are already destroying England.

The other element in the case is so very long that I will here make it very short. The Parish Constable, nominated by a District Council, is one of the very few reminders of a certain natural notion of self-government which modern science and modern discipline have made very difficult to retain. For the present I will put it merely in this way: What would any six streets in Hoxton or Whitechapel give if they could elect (however indirectly) the policeman who should stand at the street corner?

CAPONE'S PAL

I HAVE sometimes shocked the conventions of our time by defending Private Property; and pointing out that Private Property has really been destroyed by Private Enterprise. In connection with this paradox, that our common conscience does really disapprove of a thief, I came upon a very curious case the other day; an actual incident which I will leave to speak for itself. It seemed to me to combine amusement with instruction.

I had wandered out of a famous Spanish port and found myself in a sort of seaside suburb. I could not speak the language; but Latins are so intelligent that they do without language. I turned, as I had done twenty times, into a little café, which was empty, except for a sturdy man on a stool, with his broad back to me; and he jumped down with a kind of alertness which is neither Spanish nor English. He was evidently the proprietor, and he spoke English fluently, but with a blended accent I could not define; till I realized that he was not a Spaniard speaking English, but a Spaniard speaking American. Some accident of talk led me to admit that I followed the low trade of literature; whereupon he leapt into new life and proclaimed that he also had written a book. He showed me the book. It seemed to me on a hasty glance, rather a good book, written with spirit and humour; but it was simply his own memoirs as a gunman and a gangster under Al Capone. It was a perfectly honest record of dishonesty; and described robbing and racketeering without any of the cant that excuses capitalism. Still, there was something warming to a melodramatic mind in being alone with a gunman. He was dark and brooding and suddenly broke off to say, "I shan't write another book."

"No," I said applauding warmly, "keeping a bar is much better than writing a book. Many an Englishman has wished he kept a pub instead of keeping a publisher."

And at this he was transfigured into tremendous and vibrant vitality. He shouted till the tavern shook with the crimes of his publisher. He said that his publisher had cheated him at every turn. He said he had to rush round the world to see that all his publishers and translators were not doing him out of his well-earned money. I think it quite likely that they were. I also have no illusions about publishing or other phases of modern plutocracy. But I thought it was faintly ironical. I reminded him of Byron's saying that Barrabas was a publisher.

"In short," I said firmly, "it was sheer robbery."

"Sure," he said with explosive emphasis; and we parted excellent friends. "It was just Robbery!"

ON LOSING ONE'S HEAD

WHEN I was a little boy I had an imagination, though this has long been washed out of me by the wordy abstractions of politics and journalism. For imagination, real imagination, is never a vague thing of vistas. Real imagination is always materialistic; for imagination consists of images, generally graven images. There is a mad literalism about imagination; and when I had it I turned everything that any one mentioned into a concrete body and a staring shape. Thus, I would hear grown-up people using ordinary proverbs and figures of speech; pale, worn-out proverbs, battered and colourless figures of speech. But every one of these phrases sprang out for me as fierce and vivid as a motto written in fireworks. For some reason I had a particularly graphic visual concept in the case of nautical metaphors. Thus, when I heard that my uncle on a sea voyage "had got his sea legs" I pictured the most horrible bodily transformations in my uncle. Had my uncle now got four legs? Or had it been necessary for his two original and (to my eye) unobjectionable legs to be amputated by the ship's doctor? Did the new legs arrive as a sort of extra luggage, or did they loathsomely grow upon him, like hair or fungoids, with all the awful unnaturalness of Nature? I pictured my uncle's sea legs as two green and glittering members, covered with scales like fishes, and bearing some resemblance to the two fish tails with which exuberant Renaissance artists sometimes provided Tritons and mermaids. Again when I heard (in some seafaring connection) that "the Captain kept his weather eye open," I assumed with faultless infantile logic that he kept the other one quite shut. And in some dreams I rather pictured the Captain's weather eye as being some separate and eccentric kind of eye, like that of a Cyclops; an eye of blue sky or lightning that opened suddenly in his hat or his coat-tails and blazed through black fantastic tempests; a strange star of the storm.

But there were many cases, even among more terrestrial and commonplace metaphors, where the material metaphor photographed itself on my fancy. One of them was the phrase about a man "Losing his heart." A man, considered as a material envelope, seemed so securely done up that how the heart could get out of the body was a problem analogous to that of how the apple could get into the dumpling. Perhaps, I mused, the phrase about a man having his heart in his mouth might throw some light on the somewhat revolting phrase, which spoke of a man with his heart in his boots; where there was clearly no thoroughfare. From this my childish taste turned with a certain relief to the easier and more popular picture of a man losing his head; which seemed the sort of thing that might happen to anybody. Indeed, by this dream of symbolic decapitation I was much haunted in infancy and am not infrequently inspired and comforted even to this day. Whatever other metaphors may mean, this metaphor of the lost head has some primary and poetic meaning; and I have written many bad poems, bad fairy tales, and bad apologues in my industrious attempt to find it out and declare it. The connection between the animal and intellectual meaning of it became close and even confused. I vaguely thought of Charles I as having lost his head equally in both senses; which is not perhaps wholly untrue. When I read of the miracle of St. Dennis, who carried his head in his hand, it seemed to me quite a soothing and graceful proceeding, like a gentleman carrying his hat in his hand. St. Dennis did not lose his head anyhow; he carried it in his hand so as not to lose it; as ladies do their ridiculous handbags.

Indeed, this drifting and dancing dream of decapitation, in which kings and saints figured with gothic fantasticality, had a kind of allegory in the core of it. The separation of body and head is a sort of symbol of that separation of body and soul which is made by all the heresies and the sophistries, which are the nightmares of the mind. The mere materialist is a body that has lost its head; the mere spiritualist is a head that has mislaid its body. Under the same symbol can be found the old distinction between the sinner and the heretic about which theology has uttered many paradoxes, more profitable to study than some modern people fancy. For there is one kind of man who takes off his head and throws it in the gutter, who dethrones and forgets the reason that should be his ruler and witness; and the horrible headless body strides away over cities and sanctuaries, breaking them down and treading them into mire and blood. He is the criminal; but there is another figure equally sinister and strange. This man forgets his body, with all its instinctive honesties and recurrent sanities and laws of God; he leaves his body working in the fields like a slave; and the head goes away to think alone. The head, detached and dehumanized, thinks faster and faster like a clock gone mad; it is never heated by any generous blood, never softened by any healthy fatigue, never checked or warned by any of the terrible tocsins of instinct. The head thinks because it cannot do anything else; because it cannot feel or doubt or know. This man is the heretic; and in this way all the heresies were made. The anarchist goes off his head and the sophist goes off his body; I will not renew the old dispute about which is the worse amputation; but I should recommend the prudent reader to avoid both.

THE SPICE OF LIFE*

FORGIVE ME if I begin by enacting the part which I have
played at so many dinner-parties, I mean the part of the
skeleton at the feast. Pardon me if the first few words that
reach you resemble a hollow voice from the tomb. For the
truth is that the very title of this series makes me feel a little
funereal. When I was asked to speak on the Spice of Life, I am
sorry to say that the first thought that crossed my perverse
and morbid mind was that spices, as spices, are quite as much
associated with death as with life. Corpses embalmed and
preserved were always swathed amid spices; mummies
also, I suppose. I am no Egyptologist to decide the point.
But even if they were, you would hardly go sniffing round a
mummy in the British Museum, drawing deep breaths and
saying, "This is indeed the spice of life." Egypt was almost a
civilization organized as a funeral procession; it is hardly an
exaggeration to say that the living lived to serve the dead.
And yet I suppose that an actual Egyptian walking about
alive, was in no hurry to be spiced. Or take a homelier scene
nearer home. Suppose you are chased by a mad bull; we will
not debate which animal enjoys more of the spice of life; but
both at the moment will give unmistakable signs of life. But
the quadruped must wait until he is killed and cut up into
cold beef, before he can have the pride and privilege of being
spiced beef. In short, I want you to remember first of all that
there has been in history, not only the spice of life, but something else that may fairly be called the spice of death. And I

* This is the text of a broadcast talk given by G. K. Chesterton for the
British Broadcasting Corporation in their series THE SPICE OF LIFE.

mention it first because it is a sort of parable; and there are a good many things in the modern world that seem to me to be dead, not to say damned, and yet are considered very spicy.

I will not dwell on this morbid parallel. Heaven forbid that I should suggest that some ladies are rather like mummies walking about, with very beautiful faces painted on the mummy-cases: or that some young gentlemen going the pace exhibit all the culture and selective subtlety of mad bulls. I am concerned with a much more important question at the back of this one. It seems to me that a great many people, whom I am far from calling mummies or mad bulls, are at this moment paying rather too much attention to the spice of life, and rather too little attention to life. Do not misunderstand me. I am very fond of spiced beef and all the spices; I always dread that the Puritan reformers will suddenly forbid mustard and pepper as they did malt and hops; on the absurd ground that salt and mustard are as unnecessary as music. But while I resist the suggestion that we must eat beef without mustard, I do recognize that there is now a much deeper and more subtle danger that men may want to eat mustard without beef. I mean that they may lose their appetite; their appetite for beef and bread and cheese and the broad daylight of life; and depend entirely on spices and condiments. I have even been blamed for defending the spices of life against what was called the Simple Life. I have been blamed for making myself a champion of beer and skittles. Fortunately, if I was a champion of skittles, there was never any danger of my being a champion at skittles. But I have played ordinary games like skittles, always badly; but all healthy people will agree that you never enjoy a game till you enjoy being beaten at the game. I have even played golf in Scotland before Arthur Balfour brought it to England and it became a fashion and then a religion. I have been since inhibited by a difficulty in regarding a game as a

religion, and the horrid secret of my failure is that I never
could quite see the difference between cricket and golf, as I
played them when I was a boy, and puss-in-the-corner and
honey-pots as I played them when I was a child. Perhaps
those nursery games are now forgotten; anyhow, I will not
reveal what good games they were, lest they should become
fashionable. If once they were taken seriously in that most
serious world, the world of Sport, enormous results will
follow. The shops will sell a special Slipper for Hunt-the-
Slipper, or a caddy will follow the player with a bag full of
fifteen different slippers. Honey-pots will mean money-pots;
and there will be a 'corner' in puss-in-the-corner.

Anyhow, I have enjoyed like everybody else those sports
and spices of life. But I am more and more convinced that
neither in your special spices nor in mine, neither in honey-
pots nor quart-pots, neither in mustard nor in music, nor in
any other distraction from life, is the secret we are all seek-
ing, the secret of enjoying life. I am perfectly certain that all
our world will end in despair, unless there is some way of
making the mind itself, the ordinary thought we have at
ordinary times, more healthy and more happy than they
seem to be just now, to judge by most modern novels and
poems. You have to be happy in those quiet moments when
you remember that you are alive; not in those noisy moments
when you forget. Unless we can learn again to enjoy life, we
shall not long enjoy the spices of life. I once read a French
fairytale that expressed exactly what I mean. Never believe
that French wit is shallow; it is the shining surface of French
irony, which is unfathomable. It was about a pessimist poet
who decided to drown himself; and as he went down to the
river, he gave away his eyes to a blind man, his ears to a deaf
man, his legs to a lame man, and so on, up to the moment
when the reader was waiting for the splash of his suicide; but
the author wrote that this senseless trunk settled itself on the
shore and began to experience the joy of living: *la joie de*

vivre. The joy of being alive. You have to go deep, and perhaps to grow old, to know how true that story is.

If I were to ask myself where and when I have been happiest, I could of course give the obvious answers, as true of me as of everybody else; at some dance or feast of the romantic time of life; at some juvenile triumph of debate; at some sight of beautiful things in strange lands. But it is much more important to remember that I have been intensely and imaginatively happy in the queerest because the quietest places. I have been filled with life from within in a cold waiting-room in a deserted railway-junction. I have been completely alive sitting on an iron seat under an ugly lamp-post at a third-rate watering place. In short, I have experienced the mere excitement of existence in places that would commonly be called as dull as ditch-water. And by the way, is ditchwater dull? Naturalists with microscopes have told me that it teems with quiet fun. Even that proverbial phrase will prove that we cannot always trust what is proverbial, when it professes to describe what is prosaic. I doubt whether the fifteen gushing fountains to be found in your ornamental garden contain creatures so amusing as those the miscroscope reveals; like the profiles of politicians in caricature. And that is only one example out of a thousand, of the things in daily life we call dull that are not really so dull after all. And I am confident that there is no future for the modern world, unless it can understand that it has not merely to seek what is more and more exciting, but rather the yet more exciting business of discovering the excitement in things that are called dull.

What we have to teach the young man of the future, is how to enjoy himself. Until he can enjoy himself, he will grow more and more tired of enjoying everything else. What we have to teach him is to amuse himself. At this moment he is more and more dependent upon anything which he thinks will amuse him. And, to judge by the expression of his face, it does not amuse him very much. When we consider what he receives, it is indeed a most magnificent wonder and wealth and concentration of amusement. He can travel in a racing-car almost as quick as a cannon-ball; and still have his car fitted up with wireless from all the ends of the earth. He can get Vienna and Moscow; he can hear Cairo and Warsaw; and if he cannot see England, through which he happens to be travelling, that is after all a small matter. In a century, no doubt, his car will travel like a comet, and his wireless will hear the noises in the moon. But all this does not help him when the car stops; and he has to stand stamping about in a line, with nothing to think about. All this does not help him even when the wireless stops and he has to sit still in a silent car with nothing to talk about. If you consider what are the things poured into him, what are the things he receives, then indeed they are colossal cataracts of things, cosmic Niagaras that have never before poured into any human being are pouring into him. But if you consider what comes out of him, as a result of all this absorption, the result we have to record is rather serious. In the vast majority of cases, nothing. Not even conversation, as it used to be. He does not conduct long arguments, as young men did when I was young. The first and startling effect of all this noise is silence. Second, when he does have the itch to write or say something, it is always an itch in the sense of an irritation.

Everything has its better and baser form; and there is irritation and irritation. There is a great deal of difference between the irritation of Aldous Huxley and the irritation of some nasty little degenerate in a novel by Aldous Huxley. But honestly I do not think I am unfair to the whole trend of the time, if I say that it is intellectually irritated; and therefore without that sort of rich repose in the mind which I mean, when I say that a man when he is alone can be happy because he is alive. For instance, a man of genius of the same generation, for whom I have a very special admiration, is

Mr. T. S. Eliot. But nobody will deny that there was a sense in which, originally, even his inspiration was irritation. He began with pure pessimism; he has since found much finer and more subtle things; but I hardly think he has found repose. And it is just here that I will have the effrontery to distinguish between his generation and mine. It used to be thought impudent for a boy to criticize an old gentleman, it now requires far more sublime impudence for an older man to criticize a younger. Yet I will defend my own idea of the spiritual spice of life against even the spirituality that finds this ordinary life entirely without spice. I know very well that Mr. Eliot described the desolation he found more than the desolation he felt. But I think that 'The Waste Land' was at least a world in which he had wandered. And as I am describing the recent world, I may as well describe it as he has described it, in 'The Hollow Men' – though nobody would describe him as a hollow man. This is the impression of many impressions.

> This is the way the world ends
> This is the way the world ends
> This is the way the world ends
> Not with a bang but a whimper.

Now forgive me if I say, in my old-world fashion, that I'm damned if I ever felt like that. I recognize the great realities Mr. Eliot has revealed; but I do not admit that this is the deepest reality. I am ready to admit that our generation made too much of romance and comfort, but even when I was uncomfortable I was more comfortable than that. I was more comfortable on the iron seat. I was more happy in the cold waiting-room. I knew the world was perishable and would end, but I did not think it would end with a whimper, but if anything with a trump of doom. It is doubtless a grotesque spectacle that the great-grandfathers should still be dancing with indecent gaiety, when the young are so grave and sad; but in this matter of the spice of life, I will defend the spiritual appetite of my own age. I will even be so indecently frivolous as to break into song, and say to the young pessimists:—

> Some sneer; some snigger; some simper;
> In the youth where we laughed and sang,
> And *they* may end with a whimper
> But *we* will end with a bang.

ON FRAGMENTS

As I have said before I am a believer in staring blankly at things; if you do it something always happens. For instance, I am staring blankly at this sheet of paper and I firmly believe that something more or less intelligible will happen soon. Men stared at the blank blue sky and invented a million mythologies. Staring stupidly at live people is more dangerous; but even this has its fascination; and if you ever see your companion's face turned towards you with the rounded and complete expression of a congenital idiot, you may be certain again that he is nearer at that moment than at any other to knowing what you really are; which I fancy is the last thing that you desire. When we cast 'an intelligent look' (as they say in books) at a thing, it only means that we stamp our own significance upon it. When we look wisely at a post we see what we mean by a post. But when we look stupidly at a post we see what a post means.

In such a trance of divine imbecility I remember once staring at the paving-stones under my feet, until I went off into a sort of dream of paving-stones. They passed perpetually under my feet like flat and silent waves of stones, and all the time I was asking myself what they were. Street after street I passed, looking at the ground like a cow. And then it suddenly seemed to me that they were all gravestones; the gravestones of innumerable and utterly forgotten men. For under every one of them, almost certainly, there was human dust. I seemed to see fantastic epitaphs on them, commemorating the deeds of heroes who are too old and too great to be remembered. There, for instance, was the man who found fire and the man who made the first wheel; men too necessary to be ever named. There were the dim poets who gave names to the flowers, and have utterly lost their own.

And among those imaginary benefactors in all ages I seemed to see one class especially predominant. I mean the people who in the dim beginning of time united one thing artificially, but permanently, with another. What primeval priest, for instance, married bread and cheese? Who was the wild visionary (of later times) who, after ransacking all the forests, and counting all the fruits of the earth, discovered that almonds and raisins had been looking for each other since the world began? Who, above all, discovered such a thing as the happy marriage between music and literature? The men who are least known from the past are certainly the men who made this combination. And the men who are best known at the present day are certainly those who are tearing such combinations in pieces.

This is the worst element in our anarchic world of today. The whole is one vast system of separation – an enormous philosophical Divorce Court. The theory of art for art's sake, for instance, as applied to painting, was a proposal to separate a picture from the subject of the picture. Sentiment would be better without art, art would be better without sentiment. In other words, a picture would be a better picture if it were not a picture of anything. And a subject would be all the better subject if you did not paint it. Such moderns easily might, I think some moderns really have, applied the same principle to that ancient combination called a song. A very modern poet might easily say that the words would convey their own natural rhythms much better without a tune. A very modern musician might easily say that the only perfectly musical songs would be songs without words. No one has yet had the star-defying audacity to hint at a separation between bread and cheese. But we must be prepared to have it said before long by some profligate aesthete that bread would be more breadish without cheese, and that cheese would be more exquisitely and penetratingly cheesy without bread. We must be prepared, I say, for a perpetual tendency towards such cleavages; and we must be prepared to answer them by insisting on the immemorial right of mankind to perpetuate such alliances. Man has from the beginning joined spoken words to an air, and the two have grown old and wise together. Those whom man hath joined let no man sunder.

This endless process of separation of everything from everything else has a good example, for instance, in the case of religion. Religion, a human and historic religion, like Christianity or Buddhism or some great periods of Paganism was, as a matter of fact, a combination of all the important parts of life. Every one of the main human interests was in old times made a part of the creed. Every one of those human interests is now put apart by itself, as if it were a monomania like collecting stamps. A religion, as understood by humanity in the past, always consisted at least of the following elements. First, of a theory of ultimate truth and of the nature of the universe. That is now put by itself and called Metaphysics. Second, of a groping communication with some being other than man. This is now put by itself and called Psychical Research. Third, of a strict rule of behaviour, with many irritating vetoes. This is now put by itself and called Ethics. Fourth, of a certain flamboyant tendency to break out into colours and symbols, to do wild and beautiful things with flowers or with garments or with fire. This is now put by itself and called Art. Fifth, of a tendency to feel that matter and locality can be sacred, that certain soils or features of the landscape can be a part of the peace of the soul. This is now put by itself and called Patriotism. And the typically modern men are mainly proud of having thus torn up the original unity of the religious idea. Ethics for ethics' sake, and art for art's sake are like the tatters of what was once the seamless robe. They have parted his garments among them, and for his vesture they have cast lots.

THE SPICE OF LIFE

by

G. K. Chesterton

On the Essay

An extract from the last paragraph of an introductory essay to *Essays of the Year 1931–32.* Published by The Argonaut Press, 1932

173

THOUGHT AND BELIEF

175

M